Prevention's
Better Living Cookbook

by Emma Bailey
and the
Prevention Editors

Copyright, 1976
RODALE PRESS, INC.
Emmaus, PA 18049
U.S.A.
Sixth Printing 1979

Breakfast

"The Night Passeth and We Have A New Day"

A beautiful day is often greeted with groans by many a wife and mother, who, while she hurries downstairs wonders what in the world she can do to get her family to eat breakfast.

This subject of breakfast has been hammered into our minds by those who seem to think we all should start our day with the same food. No wonder wise people, of all ages rebel. Why don't we consider what the full day's requirements are and include a portion of them at our first meal? That should get us all off to a healthy, pleasant start.

For the sake of time and space, when dried fruits are mentioned please remember that those which are organically-grown and unsulphured are recommended. And the grains and cereals suggested are whole grains, home milled or stone ground.

UNCOOKED BREAKFAST MIX

Take equal portions of:
whole oats
hulled sunflower seeds
dried apples or pears
  freshly grated with their skins

cracked wheat
½ the amount of wheat germ
soya flour
corn or millet or both
honey to taste

Stir well, keep covered. This is a real favorite for in-between snacks or at bedtime. You can be as imaginative as you wish, changing the grains for rye, and wholewheat berries and adding dried banana flakes or raisins or chopped nuts. Sweeten as desired. Just be sure you mix large batches.

Should you be the fortunate owner of a home grinding mill, crack your grains as you need them. Cracked grains take a shorter time to cook than the whole grains—naturally. To three cups of boiling water use one cup freshly milled grain. If you're using a double boiler, 20 minutes will be fine. Over direct heat use a heavy pan and allow about 10 minutes, after the grain has come to a boil.

Here's a hearty blend of cereals for slow cooking.

6 cups whole-wheat berries or cracked wheat
6 cups oats
6 cups cornmeal
2 cups hulled sunflower seeds

3 cups brown rice
3 cups buckwheat
3 cups bran

Cook the whole grains overnight, using a double boiler or heavy pot. Clay pots are wonderful for overnight cookery. And if you're lucky enough to have a stove with constant heat, all the better. Leave your cereal cooking slowly at the back of the stove. Use one cup of the mix to three cups of water—or the potato water left from supper. Two cups of this mix will serve five or six. Top it with honey if desired.

3

BROWN RICE & RAISINS

One cup of brown rice steamed in two cups of boiling water in double boiler until the rice has absorbed all the liquid—about 45 minutes. Add honey. This can be cooked the night before and heated with soy or nut milk in the morning. This is one of my husband's favorites, calling it "hasty rice pudding." Also sprinkle a tablespoon of wheat germ over the honey.

Let's not overlook the old time favorites of tasty porridges.

CORNMEAL PORRIDGE

2 cups yellow, undegerminated cornmeal, mixed in 1 cup of cold water
1 teaspoon salt
3 cups potato water

While the liquid you are using comes to a boil, mix the cornmeal slowly with cold water to keep it free from lumps. Pour slowly into boiling water. Cook covered for five minutes if using direct heat, or an hour in the double boiler. Serves five-six.

OATMEAL PORRIDGE

Oatmeal is cooked by the same method, but you don't need to make a paste of the oats. Currants, raisins or any dried fruit add zest. Cook the dried fruit right along with the oats.

MILLET PUDDING

Millet pudding is made the same as cornmeal. Should you have cornmeal or millet left over, just slip it into the refrigerator for a day or two. When needed for another breakfast, cut into squares and brown. Sprinkle with cinnamon and pour honey over it all—good! And when we move along to lunch, there is another suggestion for the midday use of cooked cornmeal and millet.

Soak one cup dried apricots in two cups water overnight. In the morning stir in one cup cracked wheat or one cup wholewheat berries, cook for 20 minutes. Serves four.

Top O' The Morning
Toasts

"The first draught a man drinks ought to be for nourishment and the second for pleasure."

Should your husband, young children or teenagers, belong to that ever-enlarging circle of individuals who prefer liquids for their first meal of the day—don't despair. Instead smile, and reach for the blender, the electric mixer, or for a large bowl and the ever faithful egg beater. What you set before them will be nourishing! These I call—"Top O' The Morning Toasts."

HUNZA SHAKE—Dedicated to J. I. Rodale

2 cups of water for soaking 1 pound apricots overnight
1 tablespoon wheat germ   1 teaspoon honey

Put soaked apricots and water in which they were soaking into the blender, mixer or large bowl. Beat until smooth, add wheat germ and honey and blend. Serves three-four.

STRAWBERRY-EGG DELIGHT

2 cups soy or nut milk   1 cup fresh or frozen
2 eggs   strawberries (unsweetened)
                                          1 cup cracked ice

Blend milk and eggs with fresh or thawed strawberries. Add cracked ice and blend well. This is excellent any time of day or evening. Serves five-six.

PEACH DELIGHT

Use same recipe as for Strawberry-Egg Delight, using one-half cup fully ripe, cut-up peaches, thawed peaches or home-canned fruit.

PEANUT BUTTER DELIGHT

1 cup homemade peanut butter   2 cups nut milk
½ cup wheat germ
Blend well. Serves two-three.

CAPE COD WINE

1 cup raw cranberries   1 tablespoon honey
2 cups sweet cider
Blend well. Serves four-six.

GARDEN NECTAR

2 cups fresh tomatoes   3 sprigs parsley
1 stalk celery and its leaves   1 scallion or ½ onion
½ green pepper   2 sprigs basil
½ cup wheat germ   1 cucumber

Blend well. Serves five-six. This can be heated for a hot drink on a chilly morning.

Pancakes

Put your heavy griddle or skillet on to heat while you mix the batter. When the batter is ready, test the heat of the griddle by dropping a few drops of water on it and when the drops sputter and bounce all over, the proper temperature has been reached.

A heavy griddle doesn't require cold pressed greasing—but if you want to be on the safe side, rub it lightly with a good vegetable oil (corn, peanut, safflower, etc.).

Never have your pancake batter too thick or too thin, unless you're planning on filling them; then they must be paper thin. The batter can be dropped by the spoonful or poured from a pitcher. And do be careful not to crowd the griddle, leaving enough room for turning them over. The pancakes are ready for turning when bubbles break on the top and the edges are beginning to look dry. Once turned, allow about a minute or so to finish cooking. A broad spatula or pancake turner is required to flip them easily. Always serve AT ONCE.

Lunch

"Happy is the man with nerve sublime
to drop in just at lunch time."

Thinking about lunches brings to mind what a friend said shortly after her husband retired from his business. "I promised to love, honor and obey," she said, "but not for lunch."

Our way of life has changed so that large sections of our people no longer go home at lunchtime. Then when vacations roll around the mother despairs—or reaches for the peanut butter. Besides there's always the refrigerator to drag some limp, dry leftovers out of, and try to interest the family into eating.

Let's give this neglected meal its proper place in our planning and cooking schedules. The following recipes are simple and nourishing, yet different enough to inspire a young cook to take over while mother continues with the household chores or spends the morning shopping.

From now on, you'll see that herbs are mentioned quite frequently, so a brief word about "the cook's best friend." Please, oh, please don't shake your herb jar over the pot. By so doing the cooking steam enters the jar and weakens the flavor of these delicate, aromatic leaves. Shake the herbs into your hand and crumble gently before stirring into the food.

Add your herbs about five minutes before the end of the cooking time. This allows for the release of their characteristic flavors for your enjoyment.

EGGS

(Scrambled)

The best method is by using a double-boiler. Have the water in the lower half boiling slowly. One tablespoon oil in top section of double-boiler. Crack three eggs in a bowl, add salt, a dash of pepper and add three tablespoons water. Mix well and add to hot oil and stir gently. Allow to set without stirring again to whatever degree of moisture you prefer.

(Poached)

Just a word for the success of a good poached egg. Make sure you cook it slowly. Keep the water at the simmering stage; nothing toughens eggs like fast cooking or high heat.

OMELET

Don't let anyone frighten you from making omelets. If your first two aren't successful, try again. Take a heavy skillet and place over heat allowing it to heat through slowly until very hot. Place one tablespoon oil in skillet and tilt it so the oil coats the bottom and sides evenly.

3 eggs
2 tablespoons water
¼ teaspoon salt

1 tablespoon chopped fresh parsley or watercress or
½ tablespoon parsley flakes

Beat eggs until light and add water and salt. Pour egg mixture in skillet which is now on the lowest possible heat, let cook two or three minutes. With a spatula, lift the end of the omelet nearest you, allowing the uncooked portion of egg to run to the end of the skillet. Allow that to set and tilt eggs forward again. Gently turn the cooked portion over, sprinkle the parsley over the rest and with two spatulas roll the omelet over slowly until it's completely rolled—take your time! Let it cook for a half minute or so longer and slip onto a heated dish.

MUSHROOM OMELET

With the preceding basic recipe you can use:
One cup fresh mushrooms, do not wash. Take damp cloth or wet paper towel and wipe clean. If possible, use small mushrooms. Sauté mushrooms in vegetable oil, sprinkle garlic or onion salt and one tablespoon fresh parsley, or one-half teaspoon parsley flakes and one-half teaspoon oregano or both. Add to eggs when they are almost set, fold in half, put on hot dish and serve. This makes a lovely luncheon dish which requires only a green salad and a bit of fresh fruit for dessert.

RICE-APRICOT OMELET

One-half cup uncooked brown rice which should make one and one-half cups cooked rice. Brown rice takes about 45 minutes to cook. Put uncooked rice in two cups of boiling water, allow to cook about 45 minutes, then drain.

1½ cups cooked brown rice
½ cup soy or nut milk
2 tsps. cornstarch
¼ tsp. salt

3 eggs
1 tablespoon vegetable oil
1 cup cooked apricots

Beat whites and yolks separately. Make a sauce with the milk, cornstarch and salt. Put cooked rice in sauce and add egg yolks. Fold in well-beaten egg whites. Have your heavy skillet well heated with vegetable oil and tilt pan so sides become well coated with fat. Turn heat very low. Pour in omelet and let brown lightly until the sides set. Add one cup apricot pulp spread evenly over the omelet and fold in half. Serves four. Excellent with salad for when the "girls" come to lunch. You can cook the rice the day before (also the dried apricots) and make the omelet for Sunday morning breakfast.

SUNSHINE EGGS

Remember that cornmeal we spoke about during breakfast, and it was suggested that what was not eaten be put in the refrigerator until the day you had to serve lunch to the family? Well here is one way to serve up eggs.

Take cooked cornmeal and cut in squares about 1 inch thick. Brown in oil on one side, then remove from pan. With a spoon make a hollow in the center of the browned side of corn square and return to pan. Break one egg into each hollow: cook over low heat until egg sets—about five minutes.

EGGS AND ZUCCHINI

Take three small zucchinis about five or six inches long and not more than three or four inches in diameter; wash but do not peel. Cut in thin rounds and cook gently in vegetable oil in heavy skillet.

In a bowl beat 4 eggs
1 tablespoon chopped fresh
   parsley or 1 tablespoon parsley
   flakes

¼ teaspoon garlic salt
1 teaspoon oregano
1 teaspoon salt

Add egg mixture to cooked zucchini, stir gently not to break rounds but to allow egg to seep through. Cook slowly until firmly set without additional stirring. Season to taste. Cut in pie wedges and serve with tossed salad and herb rolls.

RICE WITH POACHED EGGS

3 cups cooked brown rice. Use one cup uncooked brown rice.
6 eggs
6 sprigs of parsley

¼ teaspoon salt
3 tablespoons wheat germ

Put rice on large fireproof platter which has been heated and make six wells for eggs in rice. Place a poached egg in each and sprinkle with salt and wheat germ. Garnish with sprigs of parsley which must also be eaten. Serves six.

SCRAMBLED EGGS AND RICE

2 cups cooked rice using 2/3 cup uncooked brown rice which you can cook in advance and save for breakfast*
3 eggs
¼ teaspoon pepper or paprika

½ teaspoon salt
1 tablespoon oil

Mix eggs, rice and salt together. Have your heavy skillet well heated with the vegetable oil. Lower heat and add rice and egg mixture. When the edges look brown, fold in half and serve. Sprinkle pepper or paprika over it all. Serves six.

*Raw brown rice triples itself during cooking.

8

ASPARAGUS AND EGGS

Steam 12 stalks of fresh asparagus. If you don't have a steamer, the same can easily be done by placing your small colander in a pot which will keep it from dropping to the bottom. Place enough water in the pot to create steam, but not so the water seeps into the colander. When water is boiling set colander with cut asparagus in pot, cover and steam until tender but not mushy—keep the vegetables chewy and firm. I cook most all of our vegetables by this method, using my colander in a regular pot which fits it perfectly.

4 eggs beaten with 1 teaspoon
  salt
1 tablespoon parsley—fresh or dried

½ teaspoon garlic salt
1 tablespoon oil

When asparagus is done, place it in skillet with a tablespoon of oil. Pour egg mixture over it and let set, cooking over very low heat. Sprinkle with parsley and garlic salt. Serve plain, or with brown rice.

TOMATOES AND EGGS

Slice up four well-ripened tomatoes into a heavy skillet in which a tablespoon of vegetable oil has been heated. Sprinkle several leaves of sweet basil and a sprig of fresh parsley over the tomatoes. Add one teaspoon salt and one-half teaspoon garlic salt or one-half an onion or one-half a clove of fresh garlic—according to your individual taste. Simmer slowly so the tomato slices will not fall apart. When well heated and bubbling, turn down heat to lowest point and drop four eggs onto tomatoes. Let cook slowly until set and serve with cornmeal muffins. This is an excellent dish and hearty enough for a supper.

BAKED POTATO OMELET

2 cups mashed white or sweet
  potatoes
1 tablespoon oil
1 tablespoon soy milk

2 eggs
salt to taste
2 tablespoons wheat germ

Mix potato and wheat germ together well; add soy milk and oil, then beaten eggs and salt. Stir well, pour into oiled pie dish and bake 20 minutes or until brown.

TUNA POLENTA

(Here again we are ready to use the cooked, undegerminated cornmeal, left over from cornmeal mush at breakfast.)

2 cups cooked cornmeal, white—or yellow
¼ cup wheat germ   1 cup fresh tomatoes
¼ cup chopped green pepper   1 onion chopped
1 can tuna fish   1 teaspoon sweet basil

Spread one cup of cornmeal on bottom of casserole. Sprinkle with half of chopped onion and half of pepper and pour one-half cup of tomatoes over this and half of sweet basil. Lay tuna fish over this and sprinkle half of wheat germ over tuna, then remaining tomatoes, onion, green pepper and sweet basil. Top it all with remaining cup of cooked cornmeal, sprinkle rest of wheat germ over cornmeal and bake at 350° for about 20 minutes or until it all bubbles. Do not drain the oil from the tuna fish, since that will act as an oil for the casserole.

Soups

"HOME-MADE SOUPS ARE THE WORTH OF THE COOK"

Save the ragged end of the roast and its gravy. Then put into a pot which will hold enough water to cover twice. Also add the outer stalks from a bunch of celery and its leaves, and onion and let it all simmer away. Here again—if you are fortunate and have a stove in your kitchen which has constant heat, you're in luck! Let the bones cook overnight on the back of the stove. If you haven't this means of cooking stock, let it simmer about two hours at low heat, once it has come to a boil. Allow to cool so you can remove the fat and there you are with a good stock which will be the base for many a delightful bowl of soup.

POULTRY STOCK

Take the raw necks, heart, gizzard and wing tips of a bird or two plus the back, saving the choice pieces for broiling, frying or roasting. Add outer stalks and leaves from a bunch of celery, onion and carrots. Put water to twice its depth of the chicken parts and let simmer about two hours. Then strain the stock and skim the fat. There you are, with a perfect chicken stock.

Remember, you can save both of these stocks in the refrigerator as the base of soups in case you haven't planned soup for this day.

The heavy vegetable soup is hearty enough to serve as the main luncheon dish. The thinner soups are good as appetizers to start off dinner.

10

TOMATO SOUP WITH BROWN RICE

This is a favorite with children at lunchtime or anytime. Two quarts soup stock, beef or chicken.

1 quart fresh tomatoes	2 stalks celery and leaves
1 small onion	½ cup carrots
1 sprig of parsley	4 sweet basil leaves
½ cup raw brown rice	

Cook all gently for two hours. Put it all through sieve and press through cone with wooden roller. Return to pot, bring to boil. Add raw brown rice and cook until tender (about 20 minutes).

CHICKEN SOUP WITH RICE

2 quarts chicken stock	1 cup chopped celery stalks
¼ cup carrots cut small	1 small onion
¼ cup brown rice	1 teaspoon salt

Put cold chicken stock, vegetables and salt into soup kettle. Let simmer until vegetables are about half done. Then add one-quarter cup uncooked brown rice and continue cooking until rice is soft. This will be a hearty dish and not thin. If the chicken stock has jellied while in refrigerator don't worry. It will melt, or you can serve it like jellied consomme´.

VEGETABLE SOUP

Use beef stock or take two pounds of lean meat and a shin bone with the meat attached. Put into kettle and let come to a full boil, then turn down and skim off fat. Add the vegetables of your choice, beginning with celery stalks and leaves, one onion, one-half cup cut-up carrots, fresh string beans and/or peas. The amount will vary according to family tastes. Allow to simmer for two hours or more.

MEATLESS VEGETABLE SOUP

1 bunch celery stalks and leaves	1 cup spinach
6 carrots	1 quart tomatoes fresh or
1 cup fresh okra	home canned
1 tablespoon sweet basil	1 cup chopped parsley
chopped	2½ quarts water

Cut vegetables fine and add to water and tomatoes. Cook until done—about 30 minutes. One cup of potatoes may be added.

11

DUTCH VEGETABLE SOUP

3 quarts stock
1 cup green split peas
1 cup yellow split peas
2 cups strained tomatoes
sprig of parsley
salt and pepper to taste

1 cup chopped cabbage
1 cup chopped celery stalks
  and leaves
1 chopped onion
3 carrots chopped fine
several leaves of sweet basil

Combine stock or water with split peas and simmer until peas are soft. Put through sieve, return to pot, and add other vegetables and cook until tender. Add salt and pepper.

SPLIT PEA SOUP

3 quarts cold water
1 ham bone
1 small onion

2 cups split peas
¼ cup diced celery
2 tablespoons soy flour

Soak peas overnight in water to cover. In the morning add three quarts cold water to ham bone. Put in vegetables and simmer slowly for four hours.

FRESH PEA AND TOMATO SOUP

4 cups fresh or home canned
  tomatoes
1 tablespoon oil
¼ cup chopped parsley

1 quart fresh peas
½ cup celery
4 sprigs of sweet basil

Cook peas in tomatoes until done. Rub through food sieve and return to pot, add other vegetables and cook 20 minutes more.

LENTIL SOUP

2 cups lentils
2 quarts cold water
2 bay leaves

salt and pepper to taste
1 onion

Soak lentils overnight. In the morning, cook lentils in two quarts cold water with seasonings for about two hours or until soft. If you wish you may sieve this soup, we prefer the lentils whole.

LIMA BEAN SOUP

1 cup dried lima beans soaked overnight in 1 quart stock or water. In the morning, add:

½ cup celery, cut-up stalks and tops
½ cup cut-up carrots
¼ cup vegetable oil
3 tablespoons parsley

2 onions
1 cup tomatoes
½ teaspoon sage

Combine and cook until tender at the simmering point. Serves six.

SPINACH SOUP MADE IN BLENDER

1 quart stock
2 tablespoons vegetable oil
1 teaspoon salt

2 lbs. washed and stemmed
  spinach
1 onion cut up fine
1 tablespoon soy flour

Blend all ingredients together. Turn mixture into pot, cover and heat thoroughly and serve with hot corn muffins or rice spoon bread.

SWEDISH FRUIT SOUP

¾ cup uncooked rice
½ cup currants
½ pound seedless raisins
½ pound honey

3 quarts boiling water
½ pound dry prunes
1 lemon
4 organic apples

Soak dried fruits one hour in warm water. Dice but do not peel apples. Use the juice and rind of one organic lemon. Mix all the ingredients and stew for one hour. DELICIOUS!! If you can't get organic produce, don't use skin.

Sandwiches

Lest we forget: these sandwiches were worked out with whole grain breads. Naturally, that makes their food value higher than average, and your folks may not eat as many—don't worry. One sandwich made with whole grain bread may take the place of two or three made from devitalized flours.

Why don't we start with the ever popular peanut butter filling and get that behind us? If you own a blender, make your own peanut butter, which is easy and very good, and will contain all the unhydrogenated fat.

Shell peanuts but do not remove the red skin. Put by small handfuls in the blender which is set at low speed. When they are powdery, mix in peanut oil or any good vegetable oil to the right consistency, add salt. If your young ones use up a jar of peanut butter within two weeks, then use wheat germ oil for about one-half of the oil.

Wheat germ oil must not be kept for more than two weeks, hence the warning. But it's very good for them if used within the proper period of freshness.

Another word for this wonderful tasting homemade peanut butter— stand the jar in which you keep it *upside-down*. That's right; in that way, the oil will be at the bottom when the jar is opened.

PEANUT BUTTER AND CARROTS

Mix grated carrots with equal part of peanut butter, moisten with a bit of salad dressing or yoghurt and spread on soy bread. Excellent for lunch boxes.

P & P

Use chunk style peanut butter with a bit of chicken or veal or lamb.

EGGS AND WATERCRESS

4 hard-cooked eggs   ½ cup homemade mayonnaise, or
1 bunch of watercress   ½ cup homemade yoghurt

If you can't get watercress, use parsley or lettuce. Chop eggs and watercress very fine, mix with mayonnaise or yoghurt.

EGGS AND BEETS

Chop as many hard-cooked eggs as needed and add chopped pickled beets. The pickled beets will make the eggs easy to spread. Add a bit of salad dressing if desired and some chopped parsley.

HIKER'S SANDWICHES

Combine baked beans or soy beans or kidney beans—in other words whatever type of cooked beans you have in the refrigerator. Add chopped onion and chopped pickles. Spread thickly on whole grain bread with lettuce between the slices. If they are planning to toast these sandwiches over an open fire, wrap the lettuce separately to be eaten out of hand or to be placed in sandwich just prior to eating.

CHICKEN AND MUSHROOMS

½ cup fresh mushrooms   1 small onion
1 cup cold chicken or turkey   chopped parsley

Cook chopped onion with mushrooms in small amount of stock. Add turkey or chicken and season to taste. Cool and spread on rice wafers.

LETTUCE SANDWICHES

Chop five or six green lettuce leaves, the greener and fresher the better, with one-half pint stuffed olives and one-half cup walnut meats or your favorite nuts. Mix with four tablespoons plain yoghurt or homemade mayonnaise.

CUCUMBERS AND RADISHES

Chop small tender cucumbers; do not peel if tender and unwaxed. Chop radishes and mix with cucumbers adding a bit of fresh garlic or garlic salt, moisten with yoghurt and spread on celery sticks.

CUCUMBERS, NUTS AND OLIVES

2 cucumbers chopped
2 cooked eggs
1 cup stuffed olives chopped

½ cup chopped pecans or almonds
½ cup chopped celery
yoghurt or homemade mayonnaise

Toss all chopped ingredients with yoghurt or homemade mayonnaise.
This is good on rice wafers, rye crisp, or turnip slices.

Salads

"THE COMMON GROWTH OF MOTHER EARTH SUFFICES ME."

Since everything must have a beginning, let's begin with the earliest salad known—the tossed greens—garnished with oil squeezed from the fruits of the olive tree, and wine vinegar from the grapes of the vine, and herbs from the field.

Tossed greens come from the lettuce family of which there are many related cousins and next of kin. The common ancestor of them seems to be the stately Romaine lettuce. Many more are known and used, to name a few: Boston, Iceberg, Buttercrunch, Oak leaf and others too numerous to mention.

Excellent cooking greens can replace or be added to other salad greens, needing only a bit of olive oil and a twist of lemon juice. They are curly endive, plain endive and escarole.

As for other salad greens, we have the sadly neglected Lamb's Quarter, spinach, turnip greens, watercress, fiddle heads, the often shunned nasturtium and the lowly dandelion that never feels shunned. Its yellow blooms reflect pure happiness.

Let's not overlook the cabbages—white, green and red. From here on, the green combinations and the many non-green additions are fuel for your imagination and salad bowl skill.

Green salads were—and still are—tossed with the simplest, most artistic of all dressings and mainly by self-judgment. The basic rule for Italian Salad dressing is:

3 parts pure olive oil
salt and pepper

1 part wine vinegar
or
fresh lemon juice

The best salad oil is olive oil. Should you for one reason or another not care for olive oil, use the vegetable oils such as corn or peanut oil, sesame or soy. Although fine oils, they lack that something that olive oil does for a tossed salad.

Be sure to use wine vinegar or cider vinegar. Do not bother with the ready-flavored vinegars. The herbs should be used by themselves, like one uses salt and pepper.

The dressing should be made fresh each time. Mix the amount you need in a cup. Sprinkle the salt and pepper and herbs you may use on top and have fun tossing the greens.

Popular salad herbs are tarragon and sweet basil. Tarragon is friendly to all greens and also complementary to whatever you may drop into the salad bowl. Use fresh tarragon if possible; the dried is also very good.

Sweet basil is gracious to all salads, and especially zestful when using fresh tomatoes. It also goes well in every tomato dish, fresh, canned or cooked. As its name in Italian implies—it's a real darling to the cook.

Thyme and rosemary also add zest to salad greens. Parsley, which is most beloved, does better in other salads.

In doing research for this cookbook, I came across interesting comments regarding lettuce which I'll share with you.

It seems lettuce has always been a kitchen-garden plant. The Hebrews eat it without preparation of any kind with the Paschal Lamb. It was a favorite of the early Greeks. During the time of Domitian, the Romans added eggs and served it as a first course to excite their appetites. Sea kale was also used for that purpose.

The botanical name of lettuce is Lactus—for the milky juices in its stalks. The ancient physicians considered it conducive to repose, claiming lettuce had a cooling and soothing effect on the digestive system.

This cooling and soothing effect may be why some folks like to finish their meal with a tossed lettuce salad. Others may feel it stimulates their appetite if eaten at the beginning of dinner. Take your choice—either way enjoy a well-tossed green salad.

Pick salad greens shortly before needed. If that is not possible, freshen them by rinsing in ice-cold water. Never soak them. Dry well and place in refrigerator. Be sure the leaves are perfectly dry before you start to cut them up.

ROMAN SALAD

Break up your favorite lettuce in a wooden bowl or glass dish. Pour Italian dressing over it all and mix well, using wooden spoon and fork. Be sure you toss it lightly so it doesn't pack—packing is murder to any salad greens. Add salt and pepper to taste and garlic salt if you like. Some people like to rub the inside of their salad bowl with a freshly cut clove of garlic.

RAW VEGETABLE SALAD

Dice fresh carrots, celery and radishes. Take tender fresh asparagus and cut in small pieces, leaving the tips whole. Set it all in bottom of bowl, pour half of your oil dressing over it and let marinate for about a half-hour. Then add your lettuce and toss thoroughly.

CUCUMBER SALAD

Slice young cucumbers very thin, place in bowl and add salt and pepper to taste. Add three tablespoons of plain yoghurt and some chopped dill. Garnish with sprigs of parsley after it has set an hour or more, then serve.

CUCUMBERS AND ONIONS

Arrange slices of cucumbers and onions with a dash of oregano between. Sprinkle top layer with garlic salt and fresh mint. Pour oil dressing with vinegar and marinate for two hours. If you wish, add one teaspoon celery seed.

BEETS AND STRING BEANS

Slice cooked beets or cut in strips, whichever suits your fancy. Cut fresh string beans in French style and cook in just enough water to cover. Better yet place your sieve over boiling water and allow beans to steam. The improved taste, color and vitamins are worth it and it's really no more trouble than the usual method of cooking. Add cold beans to cut-up beets, add chopped chives and toss with oil dressing, using wine vinegar or cider vinegar.

LETTUCE AND TOMATO SALAD

Use crisp, dry lettuce and break up. Quarter as many fresh tomatoes as you want to serve. Use oil-vinegar dressing. Toss in about six sweet basil leaves, oregano and garlic salt or cut up a clove of garlic very fine. This is a lovely salad—an all-time favorite. Use the small red cherry tomatoes whole, or the yellow pear tomato which is also small; perfect for this type salad.

VEGETABLE BOWL SALAD

Marinate the following for a half-hour or more:

6 green onions	6 radishes sliced
3 stalks chopped celery	1 cup sliced cucumbers
1 shredded carrot	½ cup raw cauliflower
1 onion sliced thin	½ cup oil-vinegar dressing

Marinate the above for a half-hour or more before the salad is to be served. When ready to serve break up a head of lettuce, add marinated ingredients and sliced tomatoes, toss lightly and serve immediately.

WINTER SALAD BOWL

½ cup cooked beets cut into strips
½ cup cooked French style beans
½ cup cooked carrots cut in circles
½ cup dried lentils or dried peas cooked

Marinate in oil-vinegar dressing adding oregano, sweet basil, and thyme to taste. Let stand for half-hour, then add lettuce and toss lightly, and salt and pepper to taste.

RED CABBAGE DRESSING

¾ cup of oil
2 beets cooked and cut up fine
1 teaspoon tarragon
salt and pepper to taste

1 onion sliced
1 teaspoon honey
1 teaspoon parsley
1 teaspoon thyme

Mix everything but the oil until well blended, then add oil slowly mixing until smooth. Makes one cup.

COOKED COLE SLAW DRESSING

3 tablespoons honey
1 cup homemade yoghurt
1 teaspoon salt

2 eggs beaten
½ cup tarragon vinegar
1 teaspoon chopped celery

Cook in top of double boiler until it has become a smooth custard. Makes about two cups.

BLENDER MAYONNAISE—ABOUT 2 CUPS

1 uncooked egg
2 tablespoons cider or tarragon
  vinegar

1 teaspoon honey
1 teaspoon salt
1¼ cups oil

Blend all but the oil. Add oil gradually and blend until thick and smooth.

SUMMER SALAD DRESSING—ABOUT 1 CUP

1 egg
½ cup chopped parsley
¼ cup chopped watercress or
  spinach
1 sprig savory

2 tablespoons vinegar
¼ cup chopped onion or
  scallion
¼ cup oil
1 teaspoon honey

Blend all in blender or in a large bowl with your beater.

HONEY-YOGHURT FRUIT SALAD DRESSING

½ cup homemade yoghurt
1 tablespoon lemon juice

½ cup honey
cinnamon, nutmeg or mace

Blend altogether well, add spices and use on fruit salad.

COOKED FRUIT SALAD DRESSING

½ cup apricot juice or any desired unsweetened fruit juice
4 tablespoons honey
2 beaten egg yolks

1 cup homemade yoghurt
cinnamon or mace and salt to taste

Use double boiler in which you mix juice, salt and honey. Add egg yolks gradually and beat well. Stir constantly until slightly thickened. Remove from heat and let cool. When cool fold in yoghurt and desired spice. Makes one and one-half cups.

OIL-LESS DRESSING

3 tablespoons vinegar
2 hard cooked eggs
1 teaspoon tarragon

garlic to taste
¼ cup homemade yoghurt
fresh basil leaves to taste

Mix and blend altogether until smooth.

VINAIGRETTE SAUCE

½ cup olive oil
1 tablespoon minced chives or
onion
1 tablespoon chopped
sweet pickle
salt, pepper and paprika

4 tablespoons tarragon
vinegar
2 tablespoons parsley
½ can chopped
pimento

Blend oil and vinegar, add remaining ingredients and chill before using.

ARTICHOKE SALAD

Put one package of frozen artichoke hearts in steamer or sieve, over boiling water; let steam until tender but not soft. This is most important, vegetables should be chewed in order to release their best flavors.

Marinate cooked artichokes in basic oil-vinegar dressing, adding one teaspoon chopped parsley, one-quarter teaspoon oregano, one-half teaspoon sweet basil and garlic salt to taste. Let marinate for one hour or more, then arrange on lettuce and pour dressing over it all.

CABBAGE SALAD

1 medium head cabbage, shredded fine
1 chopped pepper
½ cup chopped celery and leaves

½ teaspoon salt

Combine with cooked dressing and chill for about two hours, serves six to eight. If you wish, add one-half cup grated carrots and one tart apple.

TOMATO-CAULIFLOWER SALAD

3 chilled tomatoes
½ cup uncooked cauliflower

oil & vinegar dressing
watercress or lettuce

Soak cauliflower in salted water for about a half-hour. Separate into small florets. Cut tomatoes crosswise into halves and place each half upon watercress or lettuce, top with cauliflowerets and serve with oil and vinegar dressing. Serves six.

STUFFED TOMATO SALAD

6 large fresh tomatoes
2 tablespoons chopped celery
1 teaspoon onion juice or a clove of garlic chopped fine

1½ cups cooked brown rice
1 tablespoon basil

Gently scoop out center of tomatoes. Mix cooked rice and other ingredients together, stuff into tomatoes. Serve on lettuce, watercress or shredded cabbage. Serve with homemade mayonnaise. Serves six.

SPINACH SALAD

1 pound fresh picked raw
  spinach
minced clove of garlic
3 hard cooked eggs
2 tablespoons lemon juice

1 grated onion
7 tablespoons of olive
  oil or corn oil
fresh tomatoes
salt to taste

Wash and drain spinach thoroughly. Cut into bite size pieces with kitchen knife. Mix salt, garlic, onion, lemon juice and oil very well. Toss until spinach is well coated, then garnish with wedges of tomatoes and hard-cooked eggs. Serves four-six according to how many eggs you want to add.

LIMA BEAN SALAD

3 cups cooked lima beans or any beans of your choice
½ cup chopped pickle, sweet or sour according to your taste
½ cup finely chopped celery
¼ teaspoon basil
½ teaspoon garlic salt

½ cup chopped parsley
½ teaspoon oregano
½ chopped onion

Mix altogether and use the basic oil-vinegar dressing to which you have added one teaspoon prepared horseradish. Serve on salad greens.

PEANUT AND CARROT SALAD

2 cups raw grated carrots
1 tablespoon grated onion
½ cup mayonnaise (homemade)

1 cup ground nuts or peanuts
1 tablespoon parsley

Mix all ingredients. Serve on lettuce with wedges of tomatoes. Serves six.

HOT DUTCH SLAW

2 lbs. finely shredded cabbage
1 egg
1 teaspoon salt;pepper to taste

Boiling water
1 tablespoon honey
¼ cup vinegar

Shred cabbage fine, add boiling water to cover and cook about five minutes and drain. Beat egg, add honey, salt and pepper and vinegar. Heat thoroughly for five minutes. Serves six. Add one-half teaspoon caraway seeds if you like them.

CHICKEN SALAD

Cut up cold chicken or turkey or duck in cubes, making sure all gristle, skin and dry portions have been removed. To two cups diced chicken or whatever you are using, chop one cup of celery—leaves and stalks. Salt and/or garlic salt to taste. Mix with homemade mayonnaise and decorate with sliced hard-boiled eggs. This is the traditional rule—but it doesn't stop there—indeed not! Listed below are variations:

With two cups chicken or whatever you are using:

(1) one cup English walnuts which you toasted very lightly in the oven. Arrange nuts and pimento strips over salad.

(2) one-half cup sliced ripe olives or stuffed olives. One-half cup slivered almonds.

(3) one cup diced apples over which you sprinkle some lemon juice. Do not peel organic apples; mix with salad.

(4) Garnish salad with tender raw asparagus tips. Asparagus tips can be lightly cooked and added as trim.

(5) Alternate slices of tomatoes and cucumbers. You can also make a maypole effect with strips of pimento, having the strips start from the top and fanning out over the mound of salad. Put green olive slice where the pimento strips start at the top.

Place salad on bed of lettuce or in lettuce cups for individual servings.

BROCCOLI VINAIGRETTE

Pick your best broccoli with firm green florets. Place full stalks (as far as the stem is tender) in the sieve or steamer over boiling water. Steam until tender but still firm. Chill and serve with Vinaigrette Sauce.

REMOULADE SAUCE

This sauce is very good to use on fish salads and is easily made. To the recipe of Blender Mayonnaise add:

1 tablespoon chopped anchovies   1 tablespoon capers
grated garlic   1 tablespoon chopped
chopped olives   parsley
                                   fresh or dried tarragon

Mix well and use with fish salads.

ANCHOVY SAUCE

Another fish dressing is made by adding a teaspoon of anchovy paste, and a tablespoon of chopped pickled onions, and chopped parsley to homemade mayonnaise.

SALMON OR TUNA FISH MOLD

1 envelope unflavored gelatin
2 egg yolks
1 teaspoon salt
1 cup soy milk
2 tablespoons lemon juice
8-ounce can of fish

Soften gelatin in cold milk in top of double boiler. Mix egg yolks, salt and beat gently. Add small amount of soy milk to the egg mixture and return to double boiler. Cook over hot water stirring constantly, until thickened. Remove and cool. When cool, add lemon juice and flaked fish. Pour in mold and chill until firm. Serve with cucumber salad.

GRAPEFRUIT AND NUT SALAD

2½ cups grapefruit or orange sections
1 cup shredded almonds or nuts of your choice
½ cup chopped dates or chopped apricots

Use Honey-Yoghurt Fruit Salad Dressing. Serve on lettuce leaves or in cups. Serves six to eight.

FRUIT SALAD DELIGHT

1 fresh pineapple
3 oranges, peeled and sliced
2 cups fresh strawberries or fresh raspberries, and ½ cup for garnish.

Cut pineapple lengthwise and scoop out the meat into balls or cubes. Add fruit to oranges and berries, toss lightly with Honey-Yoghurt Fruit Salad Dressing or with Cooked Fruit Salad Dressing and pile mixture back into pineapple shell. Garnish with whole berries. Serves six.

MY FAVORITE FRUIT BOWL

Cut up the fresh fruit in season, chill and serve with Honey-Yoghurt Dressing. Here in Vermont where our winters are long this bowl begins with strawberries and ends with the last juicy apple and pear.

Vegetables

"In everything give thanks: for this is the will of God; and eat, that thou mayest have strength, when thou goest on thy way."

Nothing can create new friends, or produce more enemies, quicker than the word vegetables, and their uses. On one side you have the raw vegetable eaters. Across from them sit the cooked vegetable addicts, both sides equally earnest and sincere in their beliefs.

As if that isn't enough, there's the prejudiced ones; they're against all vegetables. With that small (but vocal) group, it's necessary to be: "As wise as a serpent and as harmless as a dove."

One wonders if it's the way in which vegetables have been handled— or mishandled, that causes their noses to turn skyward. Who knows?

Unless otherwise stated, the vegetables in the following recipes should be steamed. If you own a steamer fine, but don't feel you must rush out to get one. Simply take your colander, set it in a pot or kettle that has a rim which will keep the colander from dropping into the water and you're all set. See that the water doesn't come up into the colander, and cover with the proper fitting lid.

Steam the vegetables only to the tender stage—not soft—or worse yet, mushy. Steaming time varies according to the freshness of the vegetable and its size. Naturally, a whole head of cauliflower will take longer than the divided florets.

Sliced, shredded or diced vegetables take less steaming time, thus retaining much of their food values and characteristic colors.

The lemon juice which is frequently used is to replace some of the vitamin C which begins to fade out the moment vegetables are picked. Hence the plea not to pick your vegetables until near cooking time. By so doing you'll have the best possible food that nature and the grower, worked to produce for your health and enjoyment.

ASPARAGUS

One of the most delicately flavored vegetables is the asparagus. These highly esteemed green stalks, are the joy of the epicures, gracing the simplest table or the most elegant feast. To my surprise and delight I learned that our beloved lilac, and the dainty lily of the valley are cousins to the asparagus.

The early physicians encouraged the eating of asparagus as a wholesome, nutritious vegetable, excellent as a diuretic.

ASPARAGUS SUPREME

A three-pound bunch of asparagus will serve four-six people. Cut the tips in two-inch lengths or slightly shorter. Cut the stalks as far down as tender or still green. Place the stalks in colander over boiling water and let steam about 10 minutes or until about half tender, then add the tips which will need only eight to 10 minutes of steaming. Do not let them become too soft. Remove colander from over the boiling water and serve hot asparagus with Hollandaise Sauce.

HOLLANDAISE SAUCE

½ teaspoon salt
2 beaten egg yolks
½ cup boiling water

½ cup oil
juice of half a lemon
pepper to taste

Using your double boiler, pour in oil, and slowly add beaten eggs, add lemon juice and salt and pepper, then boiling water. Cook until it is a thin custard, stirring constantly.

ASPARAGUS TIPS AND FRESH PEAS

Steam one cup asparagus tips—save stalks for soup. Steam one cup freshly shelled peas. When both are steamed, mix gently together and serve with cream sauce, topped with chives and chopped parsley.

CREAM SAUCE

1 tablespoon oil
1 tablespoon soy flour

salt & pepper
1 cup of soy milk

Mix oil and flour together in the saucepan and slowly add milk to keep it lump-free, add salt and pepper. Pour over asparagus and peas and sprinkle with chives and parsley.

CREAM OF ASPARAGUS SOUP

Steam stalks from a bunch of asparagus until tender. Pass through a sieve and add a quart of chicken stock. Take two tablespoons of cornstarch, dissolved in two tablespoons cold water and add slowly to stock, cook until slightly thickened. Add salt and pepper to taste, and if possible garnish with a few steamed asparagus tips.

ASPARAGUS AND DEVILED EGGS

1 bunch asparagus
juice of 1 lemon
3 eggs—hard-boiled

1 teaspoon chopped parsley or
winter savory

Steam the stalks until half tender, add the tips and finish steaming. Have three hard boiled eggs cooked and halved. Mix the yolks with homemade mayonnaise until soft and replace in cooked whites. Garnish with some of the parsley—or winter savory. Lay hot asparagus on plates and garnish with lemon juice and chopped parsley. Serve with half an egg on each plate.

MARINATED ASPARAGUS

Steam stalks so they are still quite firm. Add tips and steam until just tender. Cool, then marinate in Italian Salad Dressing for about a half hour. Serve on lettuce with wedges of tomatoes. Sprinkle sweet basil on the tomato wedges.

ASPARAGUS LOAF

3 cups steamed asparagus stalks
   cut small
½ cup cooked brown rice
1 onion browned in 2 tablespoons
   oil

1 tablespoon lemon juice
salt and pepper to taste
2 eggs
1 teaspoon tarragon

Mix well, bake in oiled pan at 350° for about 30 minutes, serves four-six.

FREEZING ASPARAGUS

Gather your asparagus when they're at their best, meaning with closed scales, or when they first come onto the market from the local growers. Cut them into desired lengths, we like 'em the length of the container. Wash and place in blanching basket, set basket in boiling water; cover; when water returns to a boil, boil one minute. Then immediately plunge basket of asparagus into very cold water or iced water. When the stalks are cold, pack into containers and pop into freezer—it's that simple. If using open box type of container, lay them alternately, one row with tips in one direction and the second row of tips going the other way. Take care not to damage tips.

ARTICHOKES

The green artichoke is the bud of a thistle-like flower which belongs to the Cardoon family. You will hear them called French artichokes, or the globe, but they're the same by either name. Most of them coming into our markets grow along the coast of northern California. The warm sea coast is their natural growing grounds.

In shopping for them, be sure leaves are bright green and closely packed. Plan one per person. The small tender artichokes can be trimmed down to their pale green leaves and delicate hearts, for special dishes.

Starting with a full-grown one, trim off the stem close to the bottom so it will stand up when cooked. If the artichoke has little spears at the very tip of its leaves, use kitchen scissors to trim leaves off about half way down. Remove outer leaves and those which have rust spots.

Soak the artichokes in cold water to cover in which one tablespoon of lemon juice or vinegar has been added, for about a half hour. That will draw out any little insects and prevent the leaves from losing color.

Drop the artichokes into boiling water, add salt and a slice of lemon, cook uncovered for about 25 to 30 minutes. Test by pulling off an outside leaf, if it comes off easily, it's done. Remove from water, turn upside down to drain.

STUFFED ARTICHOKES

Parboil as many artichokes as you plan to serve, just long enough so the leaves can easily be pushed open. While they drain and cool, prepare the stuffing.

3 tablespoons olive oil	3 tablespoons parsley
1 cup bread crumbs with	4 green olives cut fine
¼ cup wheat germ	3 or 4 mushrooms
salt and pepper	

Saute' mushrooms in oil, add bread crumbs, olives and seasoning, mix thoroughly and let cool enough to stuff. Gently spread the leaves and spread stuffing between leaves, and press leaves back. Set them upright in casserole, brush with a little more oil and cover. Bake for 30 minutes, removing the cover for the last 15 minutes. Or place upright in pan so they won't tip and let simmer for 25 or 30 minutes adding a wee bit of water if they become dry.

25

ARTICHOKE HEARTS AND EGGS

Six small artichokes or a package of frozen artichoke hearts. If frozen are used, cook according to directions. If using fresh artichokes, buy the tender small ones and trim down to the pale leaves and cut into quarters. Then slice quarters into one-quarter inch slices. Heat one-quarter cup olive oil or a vegetable oil in saucepan, add one small onion and cook until clear. Beat four eggs adding one-half teaspoon garlic salt, two tablespoons parsley and one teaspoon of oregano, salt and pepper to taste. Put artichokes into oil, heat through then add the beaten egg mixture, cook on low heat without stirring until the bottom has browned. Gently turn out onto pie plate, then slide back into the pan to brown the other side. Cut in wedges and serve with sliced tomatoes over which sweet basil has been sprinkled.

ARTICHOKE SAUCE

1 package frozen artichoke hearts, cooked and chopped or
4 tender fresh artichokes parboiled and chopped

1 small onion	1 clove garlic or
1 tablespoon parsley	½ teaspoon garlic salt
1 cup of fresh tomatoes, or	1 teaspoon sweet basil
1 can of tomatoes	salt & pepper to taste

Heat oil in clay pot or enamel pan, stir in onion and cook until light, add sliced artichoke hearts and toss lightly. Add fresh tomatoes, and all of other ingredients. Cook slowly for about one hour. Serve over bed of green noodles or brown rice. This sauce is also very good on veal slices.

ARTICHOKE MARINADE

Cook small artichokes as usual and cut in wedges, lengthwise. Marinate in Italian Salad Dressing for at least an hour, add a tablespoon of olive oil, chopped parsley and oregano and as you arrange the artichokes on lettuce, place wedges of tomatoes along the edge. If you have the small pear tomatoes or cherry tomatoes, set them whole around the dish.

BEETS

When cooking or buying beets try to get the young ones, which are much better than the larger, older beets. Trim the young tender greens, and chop into your tossed salads or steam and serve hot. Cooked cold beets are excellent for garnishes and to add to a vegetable salad. Tiny beets are often served whole. Two pounds will serve from four-six.

WHOLE BEETS

12 or 15 tiny beets steamed whole	1 tablespoon lemon juice
2 tablespoons oil	½ teaspoon chives
1 teaspoon tarragon	½ teaspoon dill

Skin the whole beets. Put all other ingredients in to a pan and let heat, then add beets and stir them for about five minutes and serve very hot.

BEETS WITH PINEAPPLE JUICE

2½ cups or more of steamed beets sliced
2 tablespoons honey
½ cup pineapple juice and 2 tablespoons crushed pineapple
salt and pepper to taste
1½ tablespoons wheat germ
1 tablespoon oil

Heat oil in top part of double boiler. Mix honey and wheat germ, add fruit juice and cook until thick, stirring constantly. Add salt and pepper and crushed fruit, when heated add beets.

ZESTY BEETS AND EGGS

2 lbs. young beets steamed
   and sliced
sliced sweet onion
¼ teaspoon dill
parsley for garnish—and
   to be eaten

Hard cooked eggs
¼ cup olive oil or
   vegetable oil
¼ teaspoon tarragon
¼ cup cider vinegar

Mix cider vinegar, oil and spices and marinate for two hours. Cut hard cooked eggs in halves, remove the yolks and mash with one tablespoon of marinade. Put yolk mixture back into egg whites and edge the plate of beets with the eggs, garnished with the chopped parsley.

BROCCOLI

Broccoli has long been called the "snob of the cabbage family." The favorite vegetable of the Romans, this dark green, closely headed clump of unopened flowers was sadly neglected in this country for years, but two World Wars helped to establish broccoli in the hearts and gardens and stomachs of many Americans.

Pick a bunch of broccoli with tightly closed flowers, if the buds are showing a bit of yellow, the vegetable will be flavorless and tough. One pound serves two.

Cut off the stalks just below the head and peel them very thin—the stalks not the heads. The stalks are very good. Soak the broccoli in slightly salted water to remove the insects which may be there. If garden grown you may add one tablespoon of vinegar or lemon juice to the soaking water. It's better to soak in a little vinegar or lemon juice than to spray the plant—that's for sure! Broccoli doesn't take too long to steam and should be cooked until still chewy. Remember it's also good raw. Steaming time will differ, if you separate the florets it takes less time than the complete head. Steam stalks at the same time. Broccoli is very good when steamed and quickly served with Hollandaise Sauce. Or be a Roman and eat it with olive oil and lemon juice—hot or cold.

BROCCOLI STALKS

If you have been cooking several bunches of broccoli using only the heads you can now steam the peeled stalks. When stalks are still chewy remove and let cool. Marinate in Italian Dressing or serve in thin rounds with homemade mayonnaise.

BRUSSELS SPROUTS

Brussels sprouts are what some call "the baby of the cabbages." One quart of Brussels sprouts serves six.

Trim the outer leaves and soak in water with a tablespoon of lemon juice for about 30 minutes before cooking. Steam until just tender, about 10 minutes. Brussels sprouts are good steamed and served with Hollandaise Sauce.

BRUSSELS SPROUTS DELUXE

Steam one quart of Brussels sprouts until still firm, and this is important for this dish—so watch 'em. Allow to cool enough to handle easily, then making a circle of them on the plate, build the circle upward to resemble a pineapple.

BRUSSELS SPROUTS AND MUSHROOMS

Steam 1 quart of sprouts   salt and
4 tablespoons oil   lemon juice
½ lb. mushrooms   chopped parsley

Cook mushrooms in oil, add steamed Brussels sprouts and toss lightly. Serve with chopped parsley, and garnish with lemon juice.

COLD BRUSSELS SPROUTS

Cold sprouts may be marinated or served with mayonnaise as one does broccoli. They are good when added to a vegetable salad, but marinate them before adding to the salad.

CABBAGE

One of the vegetables available to us all year around is the solid head of cabbage, and we wonder if that is why it's not used as much as it could be, or as interestingly. The red, green and savoy cabbage offer many varieties of dishes. The curly-leafed savoy has a more delicate flavor and is not as heavy a head. When cooking the attractive red cabbage add a little lemon juice, or cider vinegar to help retain its color. Two pounds of cabbage will serve five or six.

At one time is was considered necessary to cook cabbage for a long time. It's been found that long cooking is what makes cabbage hard to digest; now it's suggested that cabbage not be cooked over 12 or 15 minutes.

Chopped or shredded cabbage will tender up in a very short time over boiling water, so watch it, five to eight minutes should be plenty. Allow a bit longer if it's quartered.

SWEET-SOUR CABBAGE

4 cups steamed cabbage—red
or green
3 sour apples and 1 pear
2 tablespoons honey
½ teaspoon mace

1 tablespoon celery seed
2 tablespoons oil
juice of 1 lemon
¼ cup cider
1 tablespoon caraway

While cabbage steams, blend all other ingredients in a clay pot, or a dish in which you can also serve, let it simmer for about 10 minutes, then add steamed red cabbage or the green, and mix thoroughly and serve.

SAUTEED CABBAGE

4 cups cabbage shredded and lightly steamed.
3 tablespoons oil   2 teaspoons mace

Heat oil, add mace and toss hot cabbage thoroughly. This is my favorite way with the new cabbage and the delicate savoy. Do try it please.

CAULIFLOWER

Cauliflower is another member of the cabbage family. Never overcook this dainty vegetable, that's what turns it yellow and destroys its delicate flavor.

Trim the large green leaves which protect the cauliflower and cut into quarters, florets or cook whole. Soak the vegetable in salted water for about 30 minutes before steaming. Insects love the tight florets to hide in. For four people buy a head which weighs between two and three pounds.

MARINATED CAULIFLOWER

Steam cauliflower and let cool. Then add Italian Salad Dressing to marinate for an hour or more. Steam a few small onions at the same time and add to marinade, sprinkle with tarragon, oregano and garnish with freshly chopped parsley. Makes a lovely dish on lettuce with wedges of fresh tomatoes or with whole yellow or red tomatoes. Sprinkle sweet basil over fresh tomatoes.

CARROTS

Carrots are such a delight, cooked or raw—but—please keep them out of the peas! Young carrots need only to be washed and cut in rounds or strips and steamed. Never scrape them for their goodness lies in the skin. If you steam them, you will find that the skin falls away so you haven't lost their goodness. Two pounds serves from five to six people.

It hardly seems necessary to say that fresh carrots are a must to all soups and stews, still it must be said. Carrots eaten "au jus," or straight from the garden are pure delight.

CARROTS LYONNAISE

Cut carrots in round slices, add a bay leaf and steam. Peel after they are just tender. Cook one minced onion in one tablespoon oil, add the carrots and sprinkle with thyme, parsley, salt and pepper.

LEMONED CARROTS

Cut carrots in strips and steam until tender.

2 cups of carrots	1 tablespoon honey
2 tablespoons oil	juice of half a lemon
1 tablespoon chopped parsley	1 teaspoon salt

Simmer oil and honey, add salt. Remove skins from steamed carrots and add to oil-honey mixture. Toss lightly so the carrots will all be coated, add the lemon juice and pour into serving dish, sprinkle with chopped parsley. The same can be done by using one-quarter cup of unsweetened pineapple juice in place of the lemon.

CELERY

This wonderful vegetable is one of those things—like the air we breathe—we accept it; it's always around, and somehow we don't realize its many uses. Besides filling the center stalks with cheese, and chopping the outer leaves and stalks for soup and stew, celery is a tasty side vegetable, especially with heavy meats.

STEWED CELERY

Scrub the stalks and wash the leaves of two bunches of celery. Cut the stalks into bite-sized pieces and lay the leaves on top, steam until tender. Serves two-four.

PUREE OF CELERY

One green bunch of celery	chicken stock
oil	or soy milk
mace	or nutmeg

Wash, then cut fine the stalks and leaves of celery, steam until tender. Press through the food mill, reheat by adding as much chicken stock, or milk to the desired consistency. Add oil and spices, and serve very hot.

CELERY AND CARROTS

Dice celery stalks of one bunch of celery. Save the leaves for a soup or stew. Four to six carrots depending on size, diced. Steam carrots and celery until tender. Sprinkle with parsley. This vegetable combination is good for one on a salt-free diet. Celery is tasty enough and replaces the need of salt.

CELERY-VEGETABLE BLENDER SOUP

Place leaves and stalks from one bunch of celery in blender. Add four raw carrots, one tomato, one tablespoon parsley, one tablespoon chives or small onion, blend well.

Corn

How sweet corn should be cooked can bring on as many thoughts as the kernels on the cob itself. Some folks are firm believers in starting out by placing the corn in cold water, and when the water has come to a boil, the corn is ready to be eaten—be that as it may!

We like it best when we set the water up to boil, then go out and pick the corn, leaving the last thin husk on the ear. When the water boils we drop the corn in, cooking for three minutes. That's another method—take your pick.

Since many folks buy their corn from the markets, let's say this—put your corn in a cool place—not the refrigerator—and use as soon as possible.

ROASTED CORN

Roasted corn is very good and you can roast them in their husks in a hot oven or in the hot ashes of an outdoor grill. Let them roast for a half hour. If the corn may not be as fresh as you hoped, here's a remedy. Gently turn back a little of the husks so you can sprinkle a little water from your hand onto the corn, close up tightly. The water will create steam and so tenderize the corn.

KERNELS

Eight ears of your favorite corn, be it Country Gentleman, Golden Bantam or the new midget varieties. Drop the ears on which the last thin husk remains into boiling water to cover. Let boil three minutes and remove from kettle. With a sharp knife cut the corn from the cobs. Heat four tablespoons of oil in heavy pan; gently toss the corn. Cover and let it steam a few minutes. Add salt and pepper to taste.

CORN AND TOMATOES

Cut 6 large fresh tomatoes   2 cups fresh corn cut
chives, parsley and sweet basil   from cobs

Combine the tomatoes and corn and cook gently. Add chopped chives, parsley and sweet basil, cook about 15 minutes.

SUMMER SUCCOTASH

8 to 10 fresh ears of corn, so you have 4 cups of corn off the cob
4 cups fresh shell beans   2 tablespoons oil
salt and pepper   ½ cup corn pot liquid
         or soy milk

Cut the corn off the cobs and cook the cobs in about a cup of the corn liquid. Cook the fresh shell beans until almost done. Add the corn and add if more liquid is needed, the water from the corn cobs. Cook gently for about five more minutes. Season and serve.

WINTER CORN AND BEANS

If you like lima beans and corn, this is your chance. Soak a half cup of lima beans overnight. In the morning set on back of the stove, (if you have a stove with constant heat) and cook all day slowly. If you have a modern range, cook on low heat until the lima beans are tender. About a half hour before serving time, add frozen corn. Allow corn to defrost at room temperature before adding to hot beans or the corn will be tough. Season to taste and allow to heat through.

FRESH CORN CAKES

6 to 8 ears of corn   1 egg
½ cup soy or rice flour   1 tablespoon oil
salt to taste

Cut kernels from cobs, add egg, flour, oil, and salt. Mix thoroughly until batter is smooth. Bake on hot griddle which has been slightly oiled and serve piping hot. A word of warning—make these in big batches.

SPICED CORN

2 cups fresh corn   2 tablespoons oil
1 chopped onion   ½ cup cider vinegar
2 whole cloves   chopped pimento

Heat oil and cook onion until tender. Add vinegar, cloves and stir in corn and cook slowly for about 15 minutes. Before serving remove whole cloves and stir in chopped pimento.

DANDELION GREENS

The hardy dandelion which comes early in the spring to "clear our blood" is a carefree plant. One that expresses its joy of living by covering the hills, meadows and lawns with yellow blooms. It is a tender salad green if picked early in the season. If you object to its bitterness when cooked there is a simple remedy; drain off the first cooking water then proceed to cook as planned, with a ham bone, or plain steamed with oil and lemon juice. Dandelions can also be bought in the markets, washed and packaged.

Dent-de-Lion, means tooth of the lion. Wonder how this useful and pretty plant which is brimming over with vitamin A ever acquired that name from the French?

DANDELION SALAD

Cut off the stalks, use only the tender leaves. Soak in salted water to help remove some of the bitterness. When crisp, drain and dry with paper towels. Rub the salad bowl with a clove of garlic and add greens, toss with Italian Salad Dressing. Hard cooked eggs may be quartered and added to the salad bowl.

STEAMED DANDELION

Pick over greens and soak in salted water. Using a ham bone, add an onion and when the stock is done, add the greens and cook until tender.

EGGPLANT

The beautiful, purple eggplant, is another vegetable that for a long time was not used in this country to its full potential. Now more and more people are including them in their menus, and gardeners up and down this great country are raising eggplants in their home gardens. This royal colored, bell-shaped vegetable is most adaptable for meatless meals, and a boon to the vegetarians. A one and one-half pound eggplant will serve four.

EGGPLANT-BURGERS

1 eggplant
garlic salt
2 tablespoons rye flour
½ cup bread crumbs or wheat germ

2 eggs beaten
1 tablespoon oregano
1 tablespoon parsley

Do not peel, but cut out soft spots if any. Cut in cubes and steam over boiling water until just tender. Remove colander from over hot water and let drain until no more water drips from the colander. Put in mixing bowl, add beaten eggs and other ingredients. Allow to stand so the crumbs or wheat germ have swollen and all the flavors have blended, about one-half hour. Sprinkle your hands with flour and shape mixture into burgers. Fry in hot olive oil or vegetable oil, and serve very hot. If desired serve with tomato sauce, we like 'em crisp and plain. But please—no catsup!

MUSHROOM-FILLED EGGPLANT

1 medium to large eggplant
1 pound mushrooms
1 onion

1 teaspoon parsley
4 tablespoons oil
wheat germ

Cut the top off an eggplant by following the lines of the green leaf cap. Set aside for the lid. With a sharp spoon trim out some of the pulp—but be careful, save the pulp, but not the seeds. Steam the shell over hot water, also the pulp. Do not allow the shell to become soft, just flexible. Saute' the mushrooms in oil, add the steamed pulp, and chopped onion. Fill the eggplant with the mushroom mixture, sprinkle with wheat germ and parsley, slip into hot oven until the wheat germ browns lightly and it's hot. Be sure the eggplant is in a dish which will keep it upright. Dip the lid into hot water just to heat, and take to the table wearing its cap.

If you wish, you can use hollowed-out eggplants as food cases for fish and other foods, cooking the pulp and adding to the ham, fish or what have you. Ground nuts can replace meat or fish. It seems wasteful not to use the whole vegetable so we steam the cases and eat it all, every bit!

EGGPLANT AND RICE

1 cup uncooked brown rice   1 eggplant
1 onion   2 cups tomato juice
3 tablespoons oil   sweet basil, parsley and thyme

Cook brown rice in boiling water about 30 minutes or until almost done.
Cut eggplant in small wedges and steam until just tender. Brown the onion in oil, when done remove. Lightly toss the herbs and mix the cooked rice thoroughly, add eggplant wedges. Grease a baking dish and pour in the mixture. Sprinkle with the onion and herbs. Pour tomato juice over all and bake at 350° for about 25 minutes or until nice and bubbly.

MARINATED EGGPLANT

Cut a medium eggplant in cubes or strips, about finger length and not over one-half inch thick, steam until still firm. While hot, place in Italian Salad dressing, to which you have added a chopped clove of garlic and a bit more oil, about a teaspoon oregano and parsley. Let stand an hour at least, then remove the garlic slivers and serve. If you have any left over, place in covered jar in refrigerator, it will keep very well.

Excellent with meat, especially lamb. Also good served in lettuce cups edged with wedges of fresh tomatoes sprinkled with chopped sweet basil. Strips of green or red peppers also make a good garnish.

ENDIVE

Endive, also known as Curly Endive and in some sections as Chicory, grows in flatspreading heads, with gracefully ruffled leaves. It is good in tossed salads, using their tender hearts. When lettuce is high priced endive makes a good lettuce stretcher. The green outer leaves can be cooked like spinach. Wash well and steam with the water which clings to the leaves. It does take a bit longer to cook than spinach. We like to sprinkle the hot cooked greens with olive oil, then squeeze lemon juice over it all.

ESCAROLE

Escarole is the straight hair member of the curly chicory family. This lack of beauty is more than made up by the crispness of its broad leaves. This, like its cousin Endive is excellent in tossed salads, having good tasting hearts.

The Italians make a wonderful vegetable pie with escarole leaves. For this they use the dark green leaves, saving the pale green hearts for salad.

FENNEL

Fennel belongs to the celery family. It is also known as "Italian Celery" or "Finocchio." If you like licorice, you'll like to nibble on crisp stalks of fennel. If you don't like the flavor of licorice pass up the fennel, and take a stalk of celery—it's all in the family.

34

CRISP FENNEL

Wash and trim as you do celery. Place in cold water to crisp up, wipe and dry.

DRESSED FENNEL

Steam one bunch of fennel and its root which has been sliced thin, until just tender. Cool, then marinate in Italian Dressing, adding a squeeze of lemon when served. Cut the fennel in finger strips.

JERUSALEM ARTICHOKES

Some folks wonder about the Jerusalem artichoke, often confusing it with the Globe Artichoke, to which it is *not* related. The Jerusalem Artichoke is actually the root of a sunflower plant known as the "Sunflower Artichoke." The tubers (the section eaten) are planted like potatoes, except they can be set out in the early spring or even in the fall; it's one vegetable root that withstands frost. This tuber with a nutlike flavor, can be baked, boiled or used raw, and is also used for making macaroni-style noodles and such products. It is considered starchless, storing its carbohydrates in the form of inulin, which makes this vegetable a boon for diabetics and for those who restrict their starch intake.

Wash and scrape one and one-half pounds of Jerusalem Artichokes and cook in boiling water until tender. After 15 minutes test them with a tooth pick, drain.

Take: 2 tablespoons oil   1 teaspoon cider vinegar
                                 chopped parsley

Heat oil, add vinegar and parsley, pour over sliced artichokes and serve.

KALE

Kale belongs to the cabbage family and is known as "green cabbage" growing in flat spreading bunches. This vegetable is improved by a light touch of frost. Like the lowly dandelion, kale is very high in vitamin A, which places them in a very special class.

KALE AND BROWN RICE

Steam one cup brown rice until almost tender, drain. Wash kale, strip the leaves from its hard center core. Steam until tender, drain, lay alternate layers of rice and kale in baking dish. Bake for half hour at 350°. Let the last layer be brown rice.

KOHLRABI

This vegetable with a turnip-like root is also a member of the cabbage family, and is cooked as you do cauliflower. The root is very good when sliced thin and cooked until just tender. Mix one tablespoon of oil with one tablespoon of cornstarch, add one cup of the water in which the root has been cooked, cook until smooth, add sliced kohlrabi, serve very hot.

The leaves of the kohlrabi plant can be steamed and served as a green with oil and lemon juice.

BUTTERED LEEKS

Trim the root, and cut the tips of the upper part off; if not very tender, cut down a bit further. But be sure you leave at least two inches of the stem section on. Cook as many as you plan to serve. Steam washed leeks over boiling water, until just tender. Serve with oil and a generous sprinkling of chopped parsley, and a teaspoon of chopped thyme. Good with meat. You can omit the oil and serve with yoghurt. This method is worthy of your attempt—you'll come back for more!

Legumes

Under this heading will be the dried legumes—the peas, pea beans, limas, kidney beans, lentils, black-eyed peas and soybeans. A legume is the seed of a vegetable which has pods. So all the dried beans and their related cousins will be in this chapter. Dried beans have for many, many years been known as the best source of vegetable protein. Some of the dried legumes can be cooked without soaking such as, lentils, black-eyed peas, split peas and pinto beans. If you don't have time for overnight soaking, you can buy the pre-soaked variety. Overnight soaking is best, however. Be sure you cook the beans gently in the same water. It's a good idea to add a bay leaf, salt and a clove of garlic in the soaking water to enhance the flavor. Overnight soaking requires only two to two and one-half hours cooking time. Remove garlic before cooking. One quarter of a cup of dried legumes will serve one person. Most of them double in size with soaking and please don't pour that water down the drain. In that water is much of the important nutritive value.

DRIED LEGUME SOUP

This can be made with whatever dried legume you like. Eight cups of water in which you soak two cups of whole peas, soybeans, pea beans, lima or kidney beans or whatever your family enjoys. To that add one bay leaf and a clove of garlic. In the morning put a ham bone in the water or it can be meatless and add the following:

½ cup of celery stalks and leaves   parsley
½ cup diced carrots   ½ cup chopped onion

Cover the kettle and let simmer two to three hours until the legumes are tender. Tenderness can be tried by the old art of "woofing" the beans. Place a few peas or beans on a saucer, blow across them and if they crack they are tender. The blowing is "woofing" the beans! If you like a puree of legumes, press it all through the food mill, reheat and serve. We like it with all the vegetables and beans floating around. Serves four-six and is very good.

For the vitamin program as individual as you are...

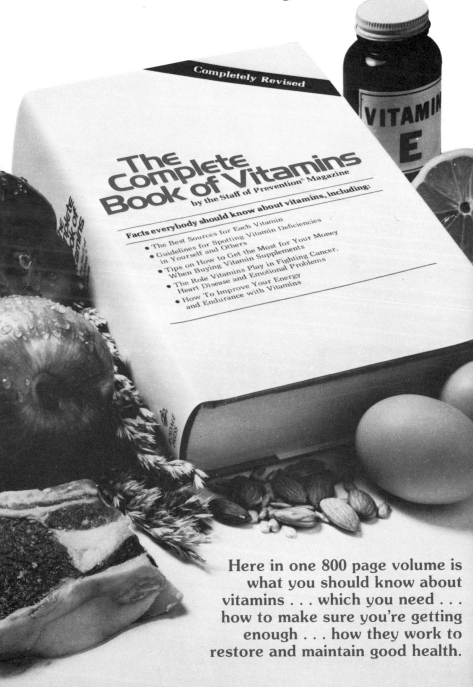

Completely Revised

The Complete Book of Vitamins
by the Staff of Prevention® Magazine

Facts everybody should know about vitamins, including:

- The Best Sources for Each Vitamin
- Guidelines for Spotting Vitamin Deficiencies in Yourself and Others
- Tips on How to Get the Most for Your Money When Buying Vitamin Supplements
- The Role Vitamins Play in Fighting Cancer. Heart Disease and Emotional Problems
- How To Improve Your Energy and Endurance with Vitamins

VITAMIN E

Here in one 800 page volume is what you should know about vitamins . . . which you need . . . how to make sure you're getting enough . . . how they work to restore and maintain good health.

Now, you and your family are invited to take the greatest single one-volume source of information about vitamins ever published.

THE COMPL
Yours FRE

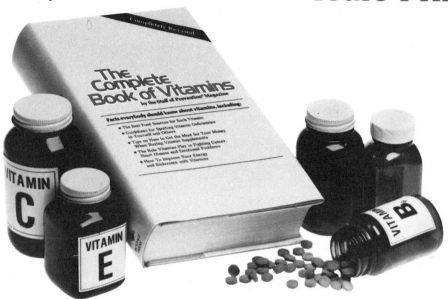

REVISED, EXPANDED EDITION

- over 800 pages
- 127 chapters
- new charts—new tables—new data

The most comprehensive vitamin guide ever published for the layman!

Some of the ailments and vitamin therapy covered in
THE COMPLETE BOOK OF VITAMINS

- The Antianemia Action of Vitamin C • Arthritics Need Vitamin C • Vitamin B6 Brings Relief from Rheumatism • An Answer for Those Aching Backs • Weak and Brittle Bones • Asthmatic Children Can Turn to Vitamin B6 for Relief • Vitamin C and Cancer • Nonsurgical Treatment of Precancerous Polyps • Vitamins Against Skin Cancer • Folic Acid Treatment Combats Circulatory Problems • Vitamin E for Varicose Veins • Vitamin E for Painful Legs and Feet • A Surgeon's Success Story: Vitamin E as a Treatment for Intermittent Claudication • Vitamin E Calms Restless Legs • Phlebitis • Vitamins That Help Clean the Blood • Niacin Therapy Lowers Blood Cholesterol • A Natural Heart Medicine • Vitamin E— The Better Treatment for Angina • Vitamins Protect Against Childhood Diseases • Vitamin E, The Other Half of Diabetes Control • B12 Prevents Tobacco Amblyopia (Tobacco Blindness) • A Nutritional Approach to Hay Fever • B6 Teams Up with Magnesium to Prevent Kidney Stones • Niacin Relieves the Misery of Migraine and Meniere's Syndrome • Pioneering Megavitamin Therapy for Schizophrenia • There's Psychotherapy in the B Vitamins • Schizophrenics—How Do They Respond to Megavitamins? • Adjusting Biochemistry with Vitamins • Vitamins Offer Hope for Autistic Children • Vitamin Treatment Reduces Learning Disabilities • The Vitamin A Effect on Acne • Vitamin E for Special Skin Problems

ETE BOOK OF VITAMINS
E for 15 days examination

WHY YOU MAY NEED EXTRA VITAMINS

Many doctors and scientists now believe "official" vitamin quotas may be inadequate for some people: that even within the same family, needs will probably differ so that what may be enough for your brother is not for you and too much for your sister.
Why?
Metabolic or digestive quirks, for example, with you from birth, may make it difficult to absorb vitamins properly. Or, if your mother was malnourished during pregnancy, you may have a vitamin deficiency you don't know

about. The way you respond to drugs and chemicals, your reaction to disease and illness, even your youthful diet may have knocked your vitamin balance out of kilter.

So though you may now eat "well balanced" meals, even take a multivitamin supplement, you may still have a vitamin deficiency that leaves you only "half well" or open to serious illness.

So find out which vitamins you should be taking. How many. How often. And why.

THREE BOOKS IN ONE

THE COMPLETE BOOK OF VITAMINS is almost like three helpful "books" in one:
BOOK I—*VITAMINS IN YOUR DAILY LIFE* explains how vitamins work in your body. You'll learn how they apparently interact and work together, why you may suffer if a link in the "vitamin chain" is missing. You'll discover how much and what kind of vitamin supplementation you may need, how to try to recognize the signs of possible vitamin deficiency and how to choose multivitamins.
BOOK II—*A GUIDE TO INDIVIDUAL VITAMINS* gives you a detailed picture of every recognized vitamin, including how it was discovered, what are its latest applications and

the foods richest in that vitamin.
You'll learn, for instance, how some researchers and physicians feel about how skin problems in some patients have responded to vitamin E; why some scientists believe vitamin C increases your brain power as it lowers your cholesterol level.
BOOK III—*VITAMIN THERAPY FOR DISEASE* covers specific ailments and conditions and describes vitamin therapy connected with these problems. You'll read about vitamins and arthritis, rheumatism, backaches, brittle bones, asthma, poor circulation, varicose veins, phlebitis, diabetes, angina and dozens of other ailments.

TAKE THE COMPLETE BOOK OF VITAMINS FOR 15 DAYS RISK FREE!

Learn how you may help both yourself and your family to life-long, good health.
THE COMPLETE BOOK OF VITAMINS is your guide to glowing, good health, and the editors of PREVENTION® want you to try it in your home for 15-days risk free. Just drop the attached card in the mail. Then, when you receive your copy of THE COMPLETE BOOK OF VITAMINS, you have 15 days to read it . . . enjoy it . . . begin to understand many fascinating facts about yourself you may never have known . . . and, above all, get a real feeling

for the kind of vitamin supplement program that is right for you and your family—to help you toward good health now and for the rest of your lives.

If, for any reason during the 15-Day trial period you decide the book is not for you, you may return it with no questions asked. You risk nothing.

So, take advantage of this special risk-free offer from the editors of PREVENTION®.

Mail in the reply card today!

YOURS FREE! When you send for your examination copy of THE COMPLETE BOOK OF VITAMINS, you'll also receive this valuable publication as a FREE gift!

The big question in life is not so much where you live . . . or how you live . . . it's how much living you do. The more you use your mind and your body, the more useful and efficient they will become—at practically any age.

"Vitamins, Your Memory and Your Mental Attitude" is an extraordinary little booklet that may serve as a truly positive force in your life—one that may show you how to increase your zest and appreciation for living —even into your older years.

It's a Free Gift from the editors of PREVENTION—yours to keep, no matter what you decide about THE COMPLETE BOOK OF VITAMINS.

15-Days Risk-Free Examination
RODALE BOOKS, EMMAUS, PA 18049

BLACK-EYED PEAS

2 cups black-eyed peas
ham bone

1 large onion
parsley

Add ham bone to the peas, cover with cold water and boil gently until peas are tender. Brown onion in vegetable oil. When peas are tender add the browned onion, garnish with chopped parsley and serve.

BEANS MARINADE

Cook the beans of your choice. Marinate in Italian oil and vinegar dressing to which you added one minced onion, parsley and oregano to taste. Let marinate for an hour or more before serving, excellent for a summer supper dish.

COUNTRYMEN'S PORRIDGE

We have a friend who makes this recipe up, and freezes it in small tins for her hiking family to take along. Reaching a place where they want to camp, the tins are removed from the knapsacks and heated over an open fire, right in their containers. A wonderful one-meal dish for those who like to snowshoe into the deep woods and build their campfires in the spotless snow.

1½ cups of dried beans (they like lima or soldier beans)
3 lbs. ham
1/3 cup yellow undegerminated cornmeal

Soak the beans overnight. In the morning cook the ham until it falls apart, remove from water and set aside. In that meat stock, cook the beans until tender or "woof" 'em.

Shred the meat and return to pot when beans are done. Mix the cornmeal with enough water until free of lumps, stirring until thick. Taste, if more seasoning is needed, add it now. This is good hot or cold. Pour into containers in which it can be both reheated and frozen. If made with dried peas, you have peas porridge hot or peas porridge cold.

LIMA BEAN CASSEROLE

2 cups dried beans or beans of
    your choice
2 cups onion
4 tablespoons oil

1 tablespoon chopped celery leaves
1 tablespoon chopped parsley
¼ teaspoon dried thyme

Cook beans which have been soaked overnight, until about tender. Brown onions in oil, add other ingredients, pour in casserole and bake about one-half hour. You may cut up left-over meat and add when ready to bake.

37

HERBED WHITE BEANS

2 cups white beans
3 tablespoons chopped parsley
3 tablespoons chopped green pepper
3 tablespoons vegetable oil

bay leaf
1 tablespoon onion
clove garlic
2 whole cloves

Soak beans with bay leaf and garlic and two whole cloves. In the morning cook in the same water until tender. Brown onion in oil, add chopped pepper and parsley, add to beans and serve. Serves four-six.

KIDNEY BEANS AND TOMATO

3 cups kidney beans
½ cup fresh or pureed tomato

1 onion
½ teaspoon basil

Cook beans with tomato and spices until tender. Place in oven to brown about one-half hour at 350°.

BLACK-EYED PEAS AND BROWN RICE

3 cups black-eyed peas cooked
1 cup cooked brown rice
1 cup diced meat

2 cups chicken
    stock
2 tablespoons chopped
    parsley

Combine cooked peas and rice with other ingredients, heat thoroughly and serve. Very hearty.

BEAN PATTIES

Use the more delicate white beans for this or you may use the beans of your choice.

2 cups cooked white beans
1 teaspoon cider vinegar
½ teaspoon oregano
1 tablespoon oil

1 tablespoon chopped onion
2 tablespoons chopped parsley
1 egg
wheat germ

Cook the beans and press through food mill while still hot, they puree much better when still hot. Add all other ingredients and form into patties, dip into beaten raw egg, then roll in wheat germ and fry in hot oil. If you prefer, oil a baking pan with vegetable oil and bake at 425° for ten minutes or until brown and turn once. Serve very hot.

SPANISH LENTILS

2 cups cooked lentils
1 cup stewed tomatoes
1 chopped green pepper
½ teaspoon sweet basil
2 tablespoons oil

1 chopped onion
1 teaspoon oregano
1 teaspoon undegerminated
    cornmeal

Combine all ingredients being careful that the cornmeal doesn't become lumpy and simmer thoroughly. Serves four-five.

MUSHROOMS

Ah, M equals mushrooms! What a versatile little vegetable, one with gigantic culinary possibilities. Mushrooms are no longer in the luxury class of eating. They are found in the stores most of the year and at reasonable prices. If you're one of those lucky people that has a bed of them in your cellar—I envy you!

Please do not peel mushrooms, much of their flavor is lost that way. Simply wipe them with a damp cloth or damp paper towel. Separate the caps gently from the stems, they break away easily and peel or scrape the stems lightly—very lightly. If the mushrooms are large or old, peel the cap skins with your fingers or a sharp knife—BUT— don't toss those peelings away—heavens NO! Barely cover with cold water and let simmer until cooked up, strain—from these peelings, you'll have a tasty mushroom stock. This stock can be used to flavor soups, stews or casseroles or in the very dish you are preparing.

These delightful morsels are low in calories, about 30 calories per cup. One pound of mushrooms serves four. Truffles are the English cousins to our mushrooms and used much in the same way. Mushrooms are the joy of Italian and French chefs—and ours!

SAUTEED MUSHROOMS

Clean and prepare 1 lb. mushrooms   1 teaspoon lemon juice
2 tablespoons olive oil   salt to taste

Rub the skillet with a clove of garlic if you like the flavor. When the oil is heated, add the mushrooms and stir until they are well coated. Add the lemon juice and cover, simmer for about five minutes. Just before serving you may add one tablespoon of cooking sherry. Garnish with chopped parsley. Serve with meat, chicken, fish or on toast.

BAKED MUSHROOM CAPS

Stem one pound of large mushrooms. Place cap down in baking dish, then sprinkle with salt and pepper, dot with two tablespoons of olive oil. Bake for 10 minutes at 425°. Perfect with steak or juicy hamburgers.

MUSHROOMS WITH HERBS

Slice 1 pound mushrooms   ¼ cup oil
1 teaspoon oregano   1 tablespoon parsley
1 chopped onion or chives   1 teaspoon marjoram

Cook onions in oil until lightly browned, add mushrooms until well coated with oil, then add one-quarter cup of stock; chicken, beef or stock from stems, and herbs. Bake in covered dish for 20 minutes at about 350°.

This is one of our favorite ways, using the dish as a vegetable with our meat or chicken.

MUSHROOMS ALA STEBBINS

1 pound mushrooms,
  remove stems from caps
4 tablespoons vegetable oil
4 tablespoons soy flour
1 cup stewed celery

¼ cup sliced stuffed olives
1 tablespoon cooking sherry
3 hard boiled eggs
salt & paprika to taste
chicken or turkey slices

Clean caps with cloth and leave whole if small or cut if large. Slice stems in circles and cover with a little more than the required one cup of stock and cook until tender, save the stems to add later. Cut the celery fine and steam with a little more than one cup of water until tender. Heat oil in pan, add mushrooms and cook about three or four minutes. Blend the flour until smooth and all mushrooms are coated with flour and oil. Stir in the mushroom stock and simmer gently, add olives when well heated and one tablespoon of cooking sherry. Garnish with egg slices and serve on chicken or turkey slices.

This is the best way to serve holiday turkey—it's more desirable than just cold turkey or dry chicken.

MUSHROOMS AS THE ANCIENT GREEKS LIKED THEM

1 pound small mushroom caps
1½ tablespoon wine vinegar
parsley, marjoram, bay leaf, tarragon and salt

¼ cup olive oil
1 clove garlic

Place oil and vinegar in sauce pan, add herbs and barely enough water to cover herbs, simmer gently. When herbs are tender, strain and let the sauce cook until it has been reduced about half; add mushrooms and cook about five minutes more, serve cold.

SPANISH MUSHROOMS

1 pound fresh mushrooms
1 tablespoon olive oil
1 cup chopped hot peppers

salt and black pepper
1 clove garlic
1 teaspoon onion

Cook the mushrooms in the oil, add the other ingredients and cook about ten minutes over very slow fire, being careful it never boils, and serve hot. If you can get the very small, whole, hot peppers cook them whole.

Onions

One of the oldest and healthiest of foods, and most indispensable to the cook is the onion. It is believed that the onion originally came from India. In Egypt it was an object of worship—why I haven't been able to find out. From Egypt the onion entered Greece and on to Italy, thence into all of Europe. In Spain a raw onion is eaten as one does a juicy apple. It seems that the warmer the climate, the sweeter the onion.

Onions have played an important part in folk medicine, where it's considered an infallible remedy for coughs and colds. Onion juice mixed with honey is all one needs to take—so I'm told. One of the fascinations of my life is folklore, after all—all the good folks had was what came from the good earth.

If you like raw onions, don't apologize; everyone will know it—but chew on raw parsley—it works — honest!

Onions should always be steamed over hot water. Cook them unpeeled in the colander over boiling water for about 30 minutes. It's the boiling of onions over direct heat that releases the sulphur compounds, which brings out the bad odor and changes the color. So remember to steam—please!

BAKED ONIONS

Steam as many large unpeeled onions as you plan to serve whole. Cut the bottoms off, and the onions will skin easily. Place in dish and serve; or place around a roast of beef, about 20 minutes before serving the meat, and baste with the beef juice. Arrange whole baked onions around the roast on serving platter.

GLAZED ONIONS

Steam 12 small onions, or as many as you want to serve. Slip skins after cutting off the bottom, and set aside.

4 tablespoons oil	½ teaspoon salt
2 tablespoons honey	

Heat the oil and honey for about a minute. Add the peeled onions and stir gently to coat them. Simmer for about 10 minutes, being careful not to scorch. Very good to serve with lamb.

ONIONS—BAKED AND STUFFED

Steam large unpeeled onions until just tender. Cut off bottoms, and squeeze out center of onions. Chop the centers into a bowl. Add wheat germ, and any left-over meat, add chopped parsley and caraway seeds and stuff the onions. Bake for three-quarters of an hour and serve with veal or chicken.

ONION SOUP EXCELLENCE

4 large yellow onions chopped	2 quarts beef stock
4 white onions grated fine	1 teaspoon pepper
2 large red onions sliced	4 tablespoons butter

Saute' chopped yellow onions in butter lightly—not browned. Pour in beef stock or water if you like it thinner, and simmer for about 10 minutes. Then add seasonings and onion rings and simmer for about 40 minutes. Serve with hot toast and grated Parmesan cheese. Serves six to eight.

41

ONION SOUP

5 onions chopped
3 tablespoons oil
1 clove garlic
3 cups stock, or half water
   and half stock

1 cup strained fresh tomatoes
2 tablespoons chopped parsley
½ teaspoon sweet basil

Brown the chopped onions in the hot oil, brown the clove of garlic at the same time, then remove. Add other ingredients, cover and simmer for a half hour.

OKRA SOUP

2 pounds lean beef cut into small pieces
2 cups okra chopped fine
1 onion chopped

4 quarts cold water
2 tablespoons oil

Brown the meat and onion in oil, add the water and let simmer about an hour and a half. Add the okra and cook about two hours longer.

STEWED OKRA

Use tender young pods and cut off the stems if you wish. Drop okra in just enough boiling water to steam them and cook about eight minutes. Drain and cook in two tablespoons oil until tender. Season with salt and pepper and serve.

SAUTEED OKRA

Wash and dry okra, cut off stems and cut crosswise. Take two tablespoons oil, add cut okra and cook gently for about 10 minutes, stirring often. Remove cover and finish cooking until okra is tender.

CREOLE OKRA

Two pounds okra washed and trimmed at the ends. Brown one onion in one tablespoon oil, add one chopped green pepper and one clove of garlic, cook all this for about 10 minutes. Now take two or three tomatoes, chop fine and add along with salt and pepper to taste. Add the okra and simmer slowly for about 20 minutes. Pour into serving dish and garnish with two tablespoons of chopped parsley.

OKRA DIP

Steam one quart of okra until tender, let cool. Use Italian Dressing, adding a bit of tarragon and marinate the okra. Or okra can be dipped into mayonnaise or Hollandaise sauce.

FRESH PEAS

Peas are one of the earliest and most beloved garden crops. Here in Vermont, one is considered a good farmer if the first crop of peas is ready on or before the 4th of July. We are indeed thankful for a cold weather crop! Peas are rich in vitamins A, B and C.

During the reign of the first Queen Elizabeth, peas were imported into England from Holland and were written up as "fit dainties for ladies, they came so far and cost so dear."

Fresh peas should be picked and shelled as near cooking time as possible for their best flavor. Never shell peas early in the morning and leave them sitting in water until you get back and start dinner; by then they have lost their flavor completely. Peas should be steamed and they take only about five to eight minutes.

FLAVORFUL PEAS

Shell two pounds of peas to serve four.

Steam over boiling water using colander or sieve until just tender, about eight minutes. Serve with a bit of freshly chopped mint. This to me is peas, as peas should be—tender and sweet.

PEAS AND LITTLE ONIONS

2 lbs. of fresh peas   6 small white onions
oil, salt and pepper   chopped parsley or mint

Steam unpeeled onions until just tender and drain. Changing the water in bottom of kettle, steam the peas over boiling water for about eight minutes. Heat two tablespoons oil in saucepan, add onions and peas and stir well, serve immediately, garnished with chopped parsley and a bit of mint, if you like mint.

PEAS COOKED WITH LETTUCE

2 cups of freshly shelled peas
Large green lettuce leaves

Place lettuce leaves in bottom of colander over boiling water, and place peas between the leaves and steam until peas are tender. Or take a full green head of lettuce and tie up the peas within the head, and steam until peas are tender. Remove from colander and place in serving dish. This is a delicious dish, do try it—please.

PARSNIPS

Do you mind if I say that parsnips are good steamed, as they should be— but—that you can also mash the steamed parsnips? Also form them into patties, and brown in oil, or you can stew them with potatoes and onions. Add a dash of parsley or cinnamon which improves them immensely. Happy eating.

POTATOES

Here is a vegetable which is so well known, so beloved, and so important to good nutrition that I'm wondering what I can say that hasn't been said.

It's difficult to believe that there's a reader who doesn't know what to do with this delicate tuber. The recipes which follow are what I think may be varied ways of using this vegetable.

The so-called Irish potato is rich in Vitamin C, and the sweet potato is high in vitamin A, both important in balancing a meal.

NEW POTATOES

This method is not new—but so wonderful that it must head the list. Wash but do not peel as many small, new potatoes as you plan to serve. Steam them over boiling water in colander or sieve until just tender but not falling apart. Add a generous amount of chopped parsley and chopped chives plus a little oil, toss the potatoes lightly in the herbs until well-coated and serve immediately.

POTATOES AS GARNISH

Scrub as many new potatoes as you plan to serve.

Steam them in their jackets until half done. Lay them around the roast you are having for dinner about a half hour before it's done and baste the potatoes with the pan juices. When serving, place the potatoes around the roast on the platter. Very good with roast beef and lamb.

SWEET POTATOES

These juicy sweet tubers can be used in many ways; baked, boiled, and also pureed for pies and puddings. Just so your sweet potatoes don't burst when you make 'em cut off a thin slice at one end before slipping them into the oven. Steam them over boiling water and mash as desired. Six medium sweet potatoes will make about two cups of mashed sweet potatoes.

They can be fried raw, cut in rounds and fried in oil until brown, sprinkle with cinnamon and serve very hot.

SWEET POTATO SPOON BREAD

4 or 5 sweet potatoes
1 cup soy milk
4 eggs
grated rind of half of
   organic orange

1½ cups honey
¾ cup oil
grated rind of 1 organic lemon
½ teaspoon cloves and
   cinnamon

Grate the well scrubbed but not peeled sweet potatoes, grate the lemon and orange. Mix eggs and honey, then add oil, mix until smooth. Add the grated potato to the mixture, then the grated lemon and orange, and spices. Oil a dish well and bake slowly for an hour at 325°. This is good served hot or cold and very good with ham or chicken.

SWEET POTATOES AND APPLES

1½ cups raw apples
3 tablespoons honey
nutmeg and cinnamon

4 cups cooked potatoes, sliced
3 tablespoons oil
½ cup water

Grease a baking dish and arrange alternate slices of apples and potatoes, dot with honey and spices. Continue in this manner until all is used. Add one-half cup water, cover and bake at 375° until apples are tender and browned. Good with roast pork.

44

PEPPERS

Peppers should have a greater use by most of us, other than for a garnish. By so doing we lose the use of a delicious vegetable, one that blends well with many other foods. Green peppers are rich in vitamin C, but the red peppers have a higher content of this valuable vitamin.

SAUTEED PEPPERS

6 large green peppers
1 chopped onion—if desired

2 tablespoons oil
salt to taste

If you object to the skins of peppers as many people do, plunge them into a kettle of boiling water for a few minutes, then peel the skin off. In a skillet brown the onion lightly, add the pepper halves or cut in quarters and cook until tender; season to taste. In place of the onion, you can brown a clove of garlic in the oil, removing it before adding the pepper.

STUFFED PEPPERS

Drop as many peppers as you plan to stuff into boiling water and parboil about five minutes, drain. When cold, cut out the seeds and fill with any of the following stuffings:

Corn And Tomato Filling

1½ cups fresh corn
¼ cup oil
½ teaspoon sweet basil

½ cup fresh tomatoes
chopped parsley
chopped chives

Mix corn and tomatoes together, add herbs and fill peppers with the filling and bake.

Soybean-Cheese Filling

½ cup raw brown rice cooked in
   1½ cups soup stock or water
1 cup cooked soybeans
½ medium onion, chopped
2 tablespoons oil (soy, safflower, or corn)

¾ cup grated sharp cheese
Soy sauce, basil, salt to taste
Topping
2-4 tablespoons grated cheese
2-4 tablespoons wheat germ

Sauté onions in oil, and combine all ingredients and stuff pepper halves. Top peppers with a mixture of wheat germ and grated cheese. Bake.

SPINACH EXCELLENCE

1 pound of garden grown spinach
1 tablespoon of olive oil
lemon juice

Steam spinach in colander over hot water or steam with the water which clings to the leaves. Steam until it has reduced to half the volume. Drain and place on hot platter, add oil and squeeze lemon juice over it all, toss lightly and serve immediately.

SPINACH WITH HERBS

Steam two pounds of spinach, drain and add two tablespoons chopped chives, two tablespoons oil, one tablespoon fresh tarragon and one tablespoon lemon juice, serve hot.

SPINACH AND EGGS

Steam 1 pound of spinach until just tender
¼ cup oil   eggs

Heat oil in skillet and add drained spinach. Arrange wells in spinach and carefully break as many eggs as you plan to serve in each nest, dust with salt and pepper. Cook slowly until eggs set to desired consistency.

SPINACH AND HARD COOKED EGGS

Steam spinach until just tender and drain, keep hot. Chop one tablespoon onion, brown in two tablespoons oil, add spinach and two cut-up hard cooked eggs. Place on platter and garnish with two more sliced eggs.

SQUASH

Both summer and winter squash are the easiest of vegetables, giving much for the little attention received. Summer squash includes the thin-skinned varieties, the white scalloped, and the dark green Zucchini—our cousin from the Mediterranean Sea.

The winter squash are the well-known acorns, butternuts, Hubbard and related species. These keep well all winter, doubling as vegetables and dessert, a staple of the hardy New Englander. Since the vitamins and minerals of this vegetable lie close to the skin, the best method of cooking is by steaming so none of their goodness is lost.

BAKED ACORN SQUASH

Wash and cut an acorn squash in half, remove seeds, rub oil over the squash meat, sprinkle with salt and pepper and bake at 375° between 30 and 45 minutes.

If you find that baking takes too long, steam the acorn squash in a little water until it feels a bit soft, then remove the seeds, oil well and bake. A half teaspoon of honey is enjoyed by some.

Acorn squash makes wonderful cases for other vegetables and meat. A meal can be made by steaming as many acorn squash as you need for serving—a half per person is usually enough if of a fair size. When just soft, remove the seeds and scoop out some of the pulp. Chop pulp with ham or chicken, add onion or chives, sprinkle with parsley, return to squash cases and bake.

ACORN SQUASH AND APPLES

Steam whole or split squash until tender. Cut up enough tart apples but do not peel—to fill the cases. Sprinkle the apples with one tablespoon of honey, one teaspoon of cinnamon and one-half teaspoon of cider vinegar or lemon juice, add to pulp. Bake at 375° until apples are soft, but not mushy.

SUMMER SQUASH AND HERBS

Use small summer squash, wash and steam whole over boiling water in a sieve or colander until just tender but not mushy. Heat two tablespoons oil, add one-half teaspoon chopped tarragon, chopped parsley, chopped chives, and pour over hot squash. Serve immediately.

WINTER SQUASH

The winter squash can be easily cooked, and please do not peel. Wash and cut a large Hubbard or Butternut, or whatever variety you like, into serving pieces—skin and all. Remove the seeds and put them out for the birds or roast in a slow oven and nibble on them in place of candy. Place the cut pieces in colander and steam over boiling water. When tender, which you test by seeing if a bit of the meat comes up easily on a spoon, remove to a hot plate and season.

Another way to prepare winter squash is to steam them in their skins until tender, scoop out the pulp and mash with a fork. Add one-quarter teaspoon salt, a sprinkle of cinnamon and one-quarter cup chopped nuts, heat in double boiler with two tablespoons oil and serve.

BAKED WINTER SQUASH

Steam over boiling water and scrape pulp from the skins, you should have about four cups of squash. Mix two tablespoons honey with three tablespoons lemon juice and one-half teaspoon nutmeg. Grease baking dish and add the squash mixture, pour honey mixture over squash. Bake at 400° for 15 minutes.

SOYBEANS

A special word about the soybean. This legume is equal to meat in food value and is starchless. Soybeans are high in proteins, the B vitamins, calcium and amino acids. This nutritious vegetable is a staple food in countries where meat and milk are scarce or high priced, supplying the humble with the same food value as the wealthy.

Because of high protein content, soybeans require a longer soaking and cooking time than other dried legumes. They should be put in the freezer overnight and soaked at least 8 hours before cooking. Boiling time will then be from 2 to 3 hours. Soybeans tend to boil over more readily than ordinary beans, so be sure to use a large enough pot and leave the lid slightly to one side until you have the heat adjusted to a simmer.

FRESH SOYBEANS

Soybeans are cooked in their pods, so you can shell 'em, then you continue cooking. Drop the soybeans into boiling water, cook about five minutes. Drain and slip the beans from their pods by pressing the pod between two fingers. Cook the shelled beans in boiling water about 10 or 15 minutes. Remember that soybeans always remain firm and chewy, they have a nice nutlike flavor.

47

SOYBEAN CAKES

2 cups cooked and mashed
  soybeans
1 stalk celery and leaves
½ cup cooked brown rice
chopped parsley

1 onion chopped
2 eggs
3 tablespoons oil
½ cup wheat germ

Add other ingredients to mashed soybeans and form into cakes. Brush broiler with oil and broil until brown on each side. Serve hot with a squeeze of lemon.

STEWED SOYBEANS

4 cups cooked soybeans
1 chopped onion
½ tablespoon parsley

1½ cups stewed tomatoes
1 tablespoon sweet basil
1 bay leaf

Mix altogether and simmer for 15 minutes or until flavors blend. Serve hot.

SOYBEANS AND EGG

4 cups mashed cooked soybeans
½ teaspoon chopped parsley
2 tablespoons wheat germ

2 tablespoons oil
½ teaspoon sweet basil
1 egg

Blend altogether well. Place in shallow, oiled baking dish so the mixture is about two inches thick. Bake very slowly at 300° for an hour and a half or until firm. Serve in hot squares. Serves four-six.

STRING OR SNAP BEANS

True, the government has been trying to have us forego the name—string beans—in favor of their suggested—snap beans. Since they labored hard and long to breed the strings out of string beans, they would like us to forget the problems our mothers and grandmothers had in stringing every fresh bean they ever cooked. So take your choice of names, but I'm talking about those wonderful bright green pods, tender and juicy, best when the tiny bean within hasn't even begun to bulge. The bigger the bulge, the tougher the pod, so beware—they've lost their "snap" by then.

STRING BEANS PERFECTO

Pick the beans when very tender or buy the small freshest ones available so they can be cooked whole or cut just once. Steam over boiling water until just tender and still chewy. Have a tablespoon of oil ready, pour over beans and serve. Add a bit of chopped rosemary and there aren't words to describe their garden goodness. The herb makes it unnecessary to add salt.

STRING BEANS AND NUT SAUCE

Steam either green or yellow beans, whole or sliced lengthwise, one pound will serve four people. While the beans steam, make the nut sauce as follows:

4 tablespoons oil   ¼ cup shredded almonds

Heat oil and add the nuts; saute' until lightly browned. Pour the sauce over the hot beans and serve. Serves four.

BEANS AND TOMATOES

For this recipe we seem to prefer the hearty Kentucky Wonders. If you cannot buy Kentucky Wonders, mature snap beans will serve very well.

1 pound of beans cut in 1 inch lengths and washed
2 cups fresh tomatoes   2 tablespoons oil
2 tablespoons chopped onion   1 teaspoon fresh sweet basil
1 teaspoon oregano

Using clay pot, or enamel or glassware, brown the onion in the hot oil, then add fresh tomatoes which have been peeled and the oregano. When the tomatoes have cooked down a little—about 15 minutes—add the beans and cook until the beans are tender. Serve with a sprig of fresh sweet basil on each serving.

STRING BEAN CASSEROLE

1 pound of green or yellow   2 tablespoons olive oil
  beans   onion rings (2 onions)
1 pound mushrooms   1 teaspoon oregano
½ cup fresh tomatoes   sweet basil
  chopped   wheat germ

Steam beans until still firm. Brown the mushrooms in the oil, add tomatoes and herbs. Grease a baking dish and lay tomato sauce with mushrooms on bottom; put on a layer of onions, then the beans, again the tomatoes, and so on, with the onion on top. Dust with wheat germ and bake until bubbly.

Lay several fresh sprigs of sweet basil around the edges and you have a pretty casserole for supper or the church buffet.

MARINATED STRING BEANS

This is one of our favorite vegetable salads, a wonderful way to use all the beans you couldn't resist picking or buying, because they were "just right."

Steam beans until quite firm. Allow to stand until slightly warm, add the Italian Salad dressing and an extra teaspoon of olive oil. Let marinate until about a half hour before serving, then add about a tablespoon of chopped chives — depends on how well you like them and how many beans you are preparing. Add chopped fresh rosemary, and chopped parsley and one teaspoon of oregano. Mound on plate and set sprigs of sweet basil around the edges.

Tomatoes

It's difficult to pinpoint where the tomato originated, but its name comes from the Mexican word, "Tomatl." The use of tomatoes as a vegetable is fairly new—dating about a hundred years or so. There are folks who cling to the fact that tomatoes are berries—either way they're an excellent source of vitamin A, B and C.

TOMATO SALAD

Pick or buy four of the freshest tomatoes possible, avoid those which are soft or overripe. Tomatoes have enough acid of their own so it's best not to use vinegar on the salad. Slice, or cut the tomatoes in wedges, pour about two tablespoons of olive oil over the tomatoes, actually olive oil is the best to use on fresh tomatoes. Mince chives very fine, or slice several small scallions, or chop a clove of garlic and sprinkle over tomatoes. Be generous with fresh leaves of sweet basil and parsley. Let set for about half hour in the refrigerator, toss again and serve. This is a fresh tomato salad at its best.

BROILED TOMATOES AND BROWN RICE

4 large firm tomatoes, red but not overripe
1 cup steamed brown rice   1 teaspoon salt
1 tablespoon chopped sweet basil   chopped parsley
2 tablespoons onion or chives

Steam brown rice until just tender, but not mushy. Mix all ingredients into hot rice—except the tomatoes. Cut each tomato in half. Place on oiled baking dish. Cover cut section well with rice mixture. Broil under moderate flame for about 15 minutes. Or bake at 375° until browned, place a sprig of fresh sweet basil on each and serve immediately.

BROILED TOMATOES WITH WHEAT GERM AND NUTS

Follow the preceding recipe using one cup of wheat germ instead of brown rice. In addition to all other ingredients, add one-quarter cup of your favorite chopped nuts.

TOMATO AND VEGETABLE GRILL

1 small eggplant   ½ " slices of tomato
sliced onions   green pepper slices

Cut small unpeeled eggplant in one-half inch slices and saute' in oil. Lay a slice of eggplant on the bottom of an oiled sheet, add a slice of tomato, one of onion and then the pepper slice. Each stack is formed this way with a sprig of sweet basil on the tomato slice. If you wish, hold the stacks together with a skewer or toothpick. Place in oven at 375° until heated through, or use the broiler with a moderate flame.

STEWED TOMATOES

Cut up fully ripe tomatoes, as many as you need. Add one cup chopped celery stalks and leaves, and one tablespoon chives or onion and one tablespoon sweet basil. Cook gently until celery is just tender, but still chewy. The tomato skins will cook off and can be easily spooned out. This is a good vegetable combination to serve with baked fish.

TOMATO SAUCE

3 or 4 cups of fully ripe tomatoes peeled and cut up
3 tablespoons olive oil or a good vegetable oil
1 clove of garlic browned in the oil and removed, or 1 small onion
   browned in oil and left in
2 tablespoons sweet basil   chopped parsley

This is the basic sauce which you cook gently for about an hour, stirring quite often. If you care to, strain, it will keep for several days in the refrigerator. This is very good if you have leftover meat which is rather dry. Heat the sauce and place the sliced meat in it, heat through and serve.

If you want a meat sauce, brown the meat with the onion or garlic, then add tomatoes and seasoning; cook until it reaches the desired consistency.

A mushroom-tomato sauce, is made the same way. Saute' the mushrooms in the oil with the garlic or onion. Add the tomatoes and herbs and cook until as thick as you desire.

TURNIPS

Turnips and turnip tops. Sadly enough, by the time turnips reach the stores their tops have been rudely torn off and thrown out. But if you have them in your garden, please steam the tops, and serve as any other green. The tops are very rich in vitamin A, B1, B2 and vitamin C — isn't it sad that the best foods are the ones we so gaily toss aside? Steam the greens and serve as a garnish with the turnip roots. Use the smaller turnips if possible, the larger ones are apt to be stringy. Two pounds of turnips or rutabagas, as they are also called, serve five or six.

STEAMED TURNIPS

If the turnips are small, and freshly picked, they need only to be scrubbed. Remove the tops and cut off the bottoms. Steam over boiling water in sieve or colander until tender.

TURNIPS WITH LEMON BUTTER

Steam turnips, which are washed and quartered, until tender. Heat two tablespoons oil, add chopped parsley, salt and pepper, and one-half tablespoon lemon juice or cider vinegar. Heat thoroughly and pour over hot turnips.

TURNIPS—BAKED WHOLE

Turnips can be baked as one does potatoes. Choose small turnips and wash them well. Bake until tender. Remove from oven and slit across top, add one teaspoon parsley and one-half tablespoon lemon juice. Serve immediately.

TURNIPS AND APPLES

1 pound turnips   3 tart apples

Peel the turnips and cut into small pieces. Steam over boiling water until soft, when turnips are almost done, add quartered apples. Remove from stove, mash turnips and apples together.

TURNIPS GLAZED WITH HONEY

6 small whole turnips   1 tablespoon oil
1 tablespoon honey   cinnamon

Steam turnips until tender, leaving them whole. Mix honey and oil in a pan, sprinkle in a bit of cinnamon, and gently turn the whole steamed turnips in the glaze until well coated. This is very good when served with lamb.

ZUCCHINI

This green summer squash is most versatile and blends well with other vegetables and eggs. Use them when they are from three to six inches long, which means they don't need to be peeled and are seedless. Should you be forced to use the larger ones, it's best to peel them as the skin is a bit tough. But do try to pick or buy them when small.

ZUCCHINI AND TOMATOES

2 small zucchini
If possible use fresh tomatoes—about 1 cup
¼ cup olive or vegetable oil   ½ cup onions or chives
¼ teaspoon dry oregano   fresh sweet basil or dried
1 teaspoon parsley

If you can use garden zucchini, tomatoes which are still warm from the sun, and fragrant fresh herbs which you picked on your way back to the kitchen, you'll have a most delicious combination of garden goodness. If you have the small zucchini, wash and slice in rounds. Saute' onions or chives in oil, add tomatoes and herbs. Add zucchini and cook gently until tender.

ZUCCHINI AND ONIONS

Wash and dice as many young zucchini as you may need.
Chop 1 or 2 cups of onion   parsley to garnish
¼ cup olive or a good vegetable oil

Saute' onions in oil until golden, add diced zucchini and cook covered for about five minutes, then remove the cover, and cook until tender. Garnish with chopped parsley and serve with meat or wonderfully alone.

Meat

"Hunger is a good cook—and won't give a week's notice."

One of the most difficult things for the young—and not so young—housewife, is shopping for the family's meat, and still keep within her food budget. She sighs at the high prices attached to the CHOICE cuts, while wondering how to make the less expensive, well-flavored grades acceptable to them.

The very best buys have long been neglected and badly misunderstood, meaning the glandular meats: kidneys, liver, brains, sweetbreads and tripe. Within this prejudiced frame are included the muscle meats: heart and tongue. And yet, with a little thought, some imagination, the skillful blending of herbs and apple cider vinegar, these nutritious cuts of meat will be enjoyed and fully appreciated.

Less expensive cuts of meat are improved by a marinade which also releases the flavors and the calcium from within the bones.

One wonders if the hurried atmosphere of our times has promoted the expensive tender cuts which are easily and quickly cooked, by sautéing, broiling, pan-broiling and roasting. The less tender meats respond well to moist, slow heat, such as stewing, pot-roasting, fricasseeing or braising, plus the artistic flair of an adventurous cook.

BUYING MEAT

1 pound of boneless meat—4 servings

The boneless meats are: tenderloin, rolled roasts, flank steak, liver, heart, brain, kidneys, and sweetbreads. For ham slices, round steaks, etc., with small bones, plan on one pound for three servings. Shoulder cuts, short ribs, and such, one pound equals two servings.

Unless you have a nice old-fashioned butcher (and I envy you if you do), most of the meats come pre-packaged; unwrap them when you get home. Set meat on a pie plate or dish, cover with wax paper and place in refrigerator. A half hour or so before cooking time, depending on the size of the meat, set out at room temperature.

It is now considered best to roast meat and fowl by low heat—from 325° to 350°—but not higher at any stage of roasting. Set roast upon rack with the fat side up and roast to desired doneness, turning once. A meat thermometer is your best insurance against an underdone or overdone roast. In the days before meat thermometers, the roast was pricked with an ice pick or similar object. If the juice was red they considered it rare. Should it run pinkish, it was medium—no color, it was overdone.

TENDERIZING MARINADE

2 cups cider vinegar ½ cup cooking oil

One bay leaf and one grated onion. Add rosemary, thyme, parsley and sweet basil. If you have these in the garden fine, if not use the dried herbs. Put the marinade in a crock or glass dish or a clay pot—not metal.

Place a three to five pound piece of chuck, a pot roast, or flank steak in the marinade, keep at room temperature turning once or twice, do this in the morning and the meat will be ready by evening. A larger piece will require overnight marinating, turn in the morning, and use for supper. Stewing meat is improved by marinating.

CHUCK ROAST MARINATED

Four or five pound piece of chuck which you had standing in the marinade for 12 hours or a bit more, drain. Place on rack and cover, roasting at 300° for two to three hours. Serve with baked potatoes and vegetables. If roast seems to be drying, add some marinade.

TASTY BEEF STEW

Two pounds beef, chuck is very good. Brown beef in fat, add six or eight small whole onions, one cup sweet cider and one-half cup water, one bay leaf, cover and let simmer for one and one-half hours. After one and one-half hours, add one-half cup diced carrots, one-half cup diced potatoes, one-quarter cup diced celery, simmer for 20 minutes and if you want to thicken the gravy, use cornstarch dissolved in cold water.

BEEF, MUSHROOM AND KIDNEY PIE

This is one way to introduce kidneys to your family. In England this is a breakfast delicacy—especially before the hunt. Take a piece of chuck, rump or round steak, about three pounds and cut into thin strips or have your butcher do it for you. The strips can be about three inches long and one inch wide, or you can cut the beef into thin cubes. Season with salt and pepper, brown quickly in oil, add one chopped onion, one-half teaspoon parsley, just barely cover with water or half apple cider and half water, simmer slowly for about an hour. When meat is tender, thicken gravy with cornstarch dissolved in cold water.

Wash and cut into rounds six lamb kidneys. Be sure you get the fat off the kidneys, sprinkle them with cider vinegar and let rest about one-half hour. Then brown kidneys quickly in a tablespoon of oil, just brown— do not cook any longer. In a baking dish, arrange beef mixture with kidney slices placed on top, more beef and more kidneys until used up. If needed add some of the pan gravy, just so it's about half-way up the dish. Add the sautéed mushrooms—about one-half cup, last, bake in hot oven at 400° for about one-half hour. Serve with a mixed vegetable salad and there you are—a wonderfully nutritious dinner and an introduction to kidneys. Serves four-six.

KIDNEYS AND RICE

4 kidneys, veal, pork or lamb   ½ cup oil
3 tablespoons cider vinegar   1 chopped onion
chopped parsley, chopped sweet basil, salt

Cut skin and fat from kidneys, slice in rounds, marinate for two hours in oil, vinegar, herb mixture. Melt four tablespoons oil in skillet and saute' the kidney slices quickly. Reduce the heat, adding three tablespoons of the marinade and cook for about 10 more minutes. Kidneys toughen with long cooking. Serve on bed of steamed brown rice. Pour some of the sauce over the rice. Serves five-six.

KIDNEYS SUPREME

1 pound lamb or veal kidneys
½ pound mushrooms
2 tablespoons chopped onion
1 cup mushroom stock,
   made from the peelings
   and stems, strained
3 tablespoons sweet cider
2 beaten egg yolks

4 tablespoons oil
½ cup chopped fresh peppers,
   half red and half green for
   color
¼ cup chopped celery
1 cup warm soy milk
3 tablespoons soy flour
   seasonings

Cut, skin and dice kidneys, sprinkle with a tablespoon vinegar, let stand while you clean and prepare the mushrooms. Saute' sliced mushrooms in two tablespoons oil for about two or three minutes. Remove and saute' the onions, peppers, and celery for two or three minutes. Add diced kidneys and brown for three minutes, add mushrooms and remove from heat. In top of double boiler, combine three tablespoons of soy flour and three of oil, blend into smooth paste, slowly add warmed milk and the strained mushroom stock, stir until smooth. Season, and when hot remove from the boiling water to cool for a few minutes, then stir in lightly beaten yolks, stir until sauce thickens. Put back over boiling water and add the kidney-vegetable mixture, heat without boiling, and add three tablespoons of sweet cider just before serving. Serve on hot biscuits or mashed potatoes. Serves four-six.

KIDNEY HASH

2 cups kidneys cooked and ground—about 6 to 8 kidneys
2 onions
1 tablespoon parsley
½ teaspoon thyme
1 egg
1½ cups cooked potatoes

1 teaspoon oregano
½ cup fresh or home canned
   tomatoes
2 tablespoons oil

Slice onions and cook in oil until golden brown. Add the kidneys and potatoes, which have been put through the food chopper, mix in egg, tomatoes and herbs and pack in oiled baking dish. Bake at 300° for 20 minutes. Serves four to six.

LIVER

If you are interested in getting as many of the important vitamins, minerals and proteins from your meat, then eat more liver. Liver it seems is one of the best blood-building, health-giving foods, and the one most shunned.

Calf's liver is the most expensive—but not necessarily the best, regarding the all-important nutrients. Beef liver, in fact, contains a higher percentage of all the essential body building elements. So—be it calf's, lamb, beef, or pork, plan to serve liver at least once a week—twice if your family will accept it graciously.

If your family simply refuses to eat liver and some do—grind a half pound of liver and mix well in a meat loaf, using one-half cup tomato in place of milk or stock and see if that isn't a good introduction. Then gradually try these recipes. By the way, 1 pound of liver serves four or five people.

LIVER AND ONIONS

True, this is not new, but well beloved, so it heads the list.

1 pound liver of your choice	½ teaspoon oregano
2 teaspoons cider vinegar	1 tablespoon oil
chopped parsley	3 large onions
salt and pepper to taste	

Cut liver in strips and sprinkle with salt and pepper. Heat oil and add sliced onions. Saute´ until golden brown. Add liver, stir well and cover. Let cook three minutes, turn slices and cook three minutes more. Sprinkle cider vinegar over all and let cook three or four minutes more, serve very hot. Remember the longer liver cooks, the tougher it becomes.

LIVER AND MUSHROOMS

1½ pounds liver	1 cup thinly sliced mushrooms
1 cup tart apple cider	3 tablespoons oil
1 tablespoon chopped parsley	1 teaspoon chopped chives
soy flour for dusting liver	

Dust liver with soy flour and brown in oil. Add the chives and parsley, and the heated cup of tart apple cider, cover it all and cook for three minutes, then remove the liver and keep hot. Add the mushrooms to the hot cider stock and simmer for three minutes, return the liver to the pan, mix well and serve very hot.

LIVER AND TOMATOES

1 pound of beef liver	1 cup sliced onions

One and one-half cups fresh stewed tomatoes, in which you cook one green pepper and one and one-half cups celery. Dust liver with rye flour and brown in three tablespoons of oil along with the onions. Add liver and onions to stewed tomatoes and simmer two more minutes. Serve with several sprigs of sweet basil floating on the top.

HEARTS

Hearts are very good as is and useful in casseroles or dishes that use ground meat or slices of meat. In most cases, your family will be receiving better nutrition from heart as an extender than from many of the other fillers used. Hearts don't need soaking or special pre-cooking treatment. When slicing a heart, cut diagonally, that seems to improve the tenderness of the meat. Wash well, cutting out the veins and arteries. Cook these scraps for your pets, they'll love 'em.

MARINATED BEEF HEART

Using a one-quarter cup Italian Salad Dressing, add another teaspoon olive oil, one-half teaspoon sweet basil, one-quarter teaspoon oregano and one teaspoon chopped parsley. Pour over slices of beef heart and let marinate about a half hour, turning now and again. Saute' slices in hot oil, cooking about five to eight minutes, depending how thin the slices are, serves six. This is an excellent dish to have for a buffet or Sunday night supper.

HEART AND BROWN RICE

Take one large beef heart which serves four.

Cut out the veins and arteries and place in baking dish, cover with two cups chopped fresh tomatoes. Pour two tablespoons oil over the tomatoes and one chopped onion, cover and bake in slow oven at 300° to 325° for about four hours. From a half to three quarters of an hour before serving, remove from oven and lay two cups cooked brown rice over the heart. Spoon the pan juice over the rice. Let bake until rice has browned. Serve with sprigs of basil and parsley around the rice.

SWEETBREADS

Sweetbreads are a delicacy with wonderful food values, coming from the throat of a young milk fed animal, mainly a calf.

After the second world conflict, a friend's son came home with a pretty war bride. While the young man completed his education, his wife stretched their food dollars every possible way. "She has taught us to appreciate sweetbreads and brains," said her mother-in-law proudly. But why didn't we ever give them a try?

Carry in mind that sweetbreads are very dainty and do not keep well. Unless you plan to use immediately, precook them, cool, and set in the refrigerator, use in a day or two. I do think it's best to precook sweetbreads anyway, it makes them easier to handle. To precook just barely cover the sweetbreads with water and one tablespoon cider or two tablespoons lemon juice. Cook slowly for 15 minutes. Cool and remove membranes. Save this pan liquor for stock to be used in the recipes of sweetbreads or brains. Brains and sweetbreads can be mixed very nicely; they are not unlike in flavor. One and one-half pounds of sweetbreads serve six.

BROWNED SWEETBREADS

Precook sweetbreads, cool and remove membrane. Season wheat germ with salt, and one-quarter teaspoon oregano. Beat one egg with two tablespoons of sweetbread liquid. Dip sweetbreads in beaten egg and back into the wheat germ. Brown in oil. Serve with wedges of fresh lemon.

CREAMED SWEETBREADS

Using precooked sweetbreads, break off in pieces. Make a cream sauce of three tablespoons oil and three tablespoons soy flour, one cup soy milk, one cup of sweetbread pan liquid, salt and pepper. Stir sauce to prevent lumps, then add sweetbreads and if you wish, some chicken. Chicken and sweetbreads are good company. Add two teaspoons sweet cider, just before serving.

SWEETBREAD AND BRAIN CASSEROLE

Precook one pound of sweetbreads and one-half pound brains in the same water. Cook slowly, and don't throw out liquid. Fast cooking toughens brains like it toughens eggs. Roll sweetbreads and brains in rye or barley flour. Brown gently in two tablespoons oil, and place in baking dish. Add two cups stock to the pan and scrape down the sides to get all the goodness. Add one tablespoon chopped parsley. Pour over sweetbreads and bake at 350° for about 20 minutes. Serves four to six.

SWEETBREADS FOR SALAD

One pound sweetbreads or one-half sweetbreads and one-half chicken, or veal. Precook sweetbreads until quite tender, cool well before making into salad. Chop one-half cup apples or pears and sprinkle with one and one-half teaspoons lemon juice to keep from turning dark. Chop one tablespoon celery stalk and leaves, and one tablespoon parsley. Mix all ingredients with three-quarters cup of homemade mayonnaise and chill well. Sprinkle nuts which have been chopped very fine on top and serve with lettuce.

BRAINS

Brains from any animal can be used, it's a matter of what the butcher has, and you'll gain stature in his sight when you ask for this excellent organ. Brains should be pre-cooked like sweetbreads. Cook slowly in water to cover, add one tablespoon of cider vinegar; the secret is in the word "slowly" for brains like eggs are spoiled by high heat. Save the stock, it's chuck full of vitamin B. Use in soup or gravies.

BRAINS AND BROWN RICE

1½ pounds pre-cooked brains   ¼ cup stock
2 cups cooked brown rice   ½ tablespoon
2 tablespoons oil   chopped onions
3 tablespoons chopped parsley

Grease baking dish and arrange a layer of rice, then a layer of brains. Repeat having rice on top. Mix other ingredients and pour over all, cover and bake at 300° for about 20 minutes. Last few minutes, uncover and slip under broiler to brown. Serves four to six.

BRAINS WITH PEPPERS AND TOMATOES

1½ pounds of pre-cooked brains   1 teaspoon oregano
3 tablespoons oil   1 teaspoon parsley
3 fresh green peppers sliced thin   1 bay leaf
2 cups fresh tomatoes stewed and   1 onion chopped
    strained   1 teaspoon sweet basil

Heat oil in skillet and lightly brown chopped onions, add peppers and cook until tender. Add stewed tomatoes and herbs, cover and simmer for about 20 minutes, then add brains and let cook very gently about five minutes more. Serve with fresh sprigs of basil or dust with dried sweet basil. Serves six.

TONGUE

True, tongue is not an organ, it's a well-used muscle, but in thinking of organ meats, tongue somehow gets included. Beef tongue is much larger than those from veal or lamb; the smaller tongues are excellent and should be used more often. Beef tongue can be bought smoked, corned or fresh, while the smaller ones generally are uncured. Smoked tongue may be salty, needing to be soaked in cold water, so be sure you read the label; that will help you decide if you should soak it or not. For safety sake, remember that no label on smoked tongue may mean it better be soaked. Allow about one-half pound per person.

TONGUE CURRY SAUCE

3 tablespoons oil   2 cups tongue stock
3 tablespoons soy flour   1 to 3 teaspoons curry powder
1 teaspoon lemon juice   1 teaspoon finely chopped onion

Heat oil, and blend with flour until smooth. Add the warm tongue stock and cook until just thick, add other ingredients and blend well, serve with cold tongue.

If in your section of the country precooked fresh tripe is available, fine! But here in Vermont, we're not that fortunate—the pickled variety is the only kind to be bought. True, pickled tripe can be parboiled, then cooked as the unpickled tripe, but it does seem to affect the flavor (to me anyway). Parboiled tripe will keep in the refrigerator, so precook a large quantity or freeze, having it ready to prepare any time.

BAKED CALF'S TONGUE

Parboil calf's tongue for about 15 minutes in water along with one onion, a bay leaf and one teaspoon lemon juice. Skin and lay tongue in baking dish; put about one-half cup of the pan liquid over the tongue and bake at 350° about 20 minutes. Serve hot in the same juices.

TRIPE—COUNTRY STYLE

This makes a good dish for a cold day with corn pone and fruit, and the meal's done—a most nutritious one at that.

2 lbs. prepared tripe cut into small squares or diced

1 tablespoon oil	1 tablespoon soy flour
1 tablespoon chopped parsley	chopped onion
1 cup soup stock	cornstarch

Brown onions lightly in oil. Add the precooked cut up tripe and brown lightly, adding one cup of soup stock slowly, keeping it smooth, if necessary add more stock. Thicken with cornstarch dissolved in cold water. Simmer for about 20 minutes, be sure it never boils, keep to simmering point and stir often. Serve very hot with chopped parsley floating on the top of the dish—wonderful! Serves six-eight.

TRIPE WITH TOMATOES

This too can be a one-dish meal, needing only a salad, dessert, fruit or pudding.

2 lbs. tripe	10 fresh tomatoes
2 tablespoons oil	2 onions
1 clove of fresh garlic	

bay leaf, oregano and sweet basil to taste—but heavier with the basil

Cut parboiled tripe into two inch pieces. Brown the onions and garlic lightly in the oil, remove the garlic and toss out. Add the fresh tomatoes which are cut up, and the herbs, cook about 10 minutes. Add the tripe and cook for another 20 to 25 minutes. Serve very hot. Cook in glass or clay or enamel pan.

OXTAILS

Just how does one classify a tail, other than calling a tail a tail? It's not an organ or a muscle, but it's mighty delicious—try it!

OXTAIL SOUP

4 pounds oxtails	1 cup fresh tomatoes
½ cup celery stalks and leaves	½ cup diced carrots
¼ cup uncooked brown rice	1 chopped onion

Disjoint oxtails and place in soup kettle, let simmer slowly and skim off fat when it rises to the top. When most of the fat has been removed, add the vegetables, rice and cook gently until tender, about two hours.

OXTAILS AND MUSHROOMS

Three pounds of oxtails will serve four to six

3 pounds oxtails	4 tablespoons soy or
4 tablespoons oil	rice flour
½ cup mushrooms sliced thin	2 cups tomatoes
½ cup diced carrots	½ cup onions
1 teaspoon sweet basil	½ cup chopped celery

Heat oil and lightly brown the onions, celery, mushrooms, cook three minutes. Trim fat from oxtails and roll in flour, add to vegetables and brown lightly. Add two cups tomatoes and cook gently for about three hours.

VEAL

Veal being an immature meat, requires longer cooking than beef. Veal should be roasted at low temperatures, not over 300°, and should not be seared. Allow 25 to 30 minutes per pound.

A leg of veal is the best buy—having unlimited uses. To begin with, veal cutlets will not be expensive, if you buy a leg of veal. You have made a wise buy, for that leg of veal represents several meals, all reasonable. (Veal cutlets cost three times as much when bought by the slice.) Besides, there are the small pieces which are perfect for the recipes that follow, and let's not forget the bones, which are wonderful for stews or broth. So keep a sharp lookout when your market has a veal special—that leg's a buy.

VEAL CUTLETS

Cut veal not over one-half inch thick, and a bit thinner if possible. About a cup of wheat germ to which you add: salt, pepper, one-half teaspoon rosemary and one-half teaspoon oregano and one-quarter teaspoon garlic salt. One egg in which you beat two tablespoons water. The cutlets can be broiled under a low flame. Roll the cutlets first in the wheat germ then dip in egg and again roll in wheat germ. It's a good idea if you allow the breaded meat to rest in the refrigerator for a half hour, before broiling. Serve with chopped parsley or lemon wedges.

VEAL AND MUSHROOMS

1½ pounds of veal cut into cubes	½ lb. sliced mushrooms
3 tablespoons oil	1 cup tart apple cider
2 teaspoons chopped parsley	¼ teaspoon oregano

Brown the veal cubes in the oil   add onions and let cook for a few minutes, turn into a casserole. Add a cup of water to skillet and stir it well and add to casserole, scraping in the bits of meat and onions. Add the seasonings, except mushrooms, cover and bake in slow oven for about an hour. During the last 15 minutes, brown the mushrooms and add to the veal. Serves four-six.

VEAL RUMP POT ROAST

Have a rump, boned and rolled, save the bones for soup or stock. In heavy Dutch oven, heat one cup tart apple cider and turn veal roast around and over until well moistened. Turn the heat very low. In double boiler heat three-quarters cup sour cream and slowly add to veal roast. Cover and simmer slowly for two hours or slip the covered pan in a very slow oven 250° for the same length of time. Remember the secret is in the low heat.

VEAL SUGGESTIONS

The breast of veal can be stuffed with a rice dressing.

Veal loaf is easily made; for flavor, add a one-half pound of ground pork. Nutmeg is a natural flavoring for veal.

As veal stew is made as other stew, add tart cider to the gravy. Serve with brown rice.

Cold veal makes a very good salad, combining with herbs, chopped onion and homemade mayonnaise which has been mixed with yoghurt. Also grind cold veal and mix with pickles or cold beets for sandwiches.

LAMB

Spring lamb is always considered the best, and is at its best when roasted. Lamb should be roasted at 300°. Do not cook until dry, it should be a bit moist—to bring out its best flavors.

LAMB ROAST

Take a leg of lamb and rub all over with the cut side of a clove of garlic. Do not cover the roast, bake at 300° allowing 30 to 35 minutes per pound. Serve with mint sauce.

Mint sauce: To one-quarter cup oil, add one-quarter cup finely-chopped mint leaves; chill and serve.

LAMB MARINADE

Leg of lamb	2 cloves garlic
1 tablespoon oregano	3 tablespoons oil
2 tablespoons cider vinegar	fresh mint leaves

Mash or chop the garlic fine. Make small slashes in the skin of the lamb. Mix oil and vinegar and herbs, pour over the leg of lamb and let stand overnight. Set the lamb on a rack and bake uncovered in slow oven 300°, 30 minutes per pound.

LAMB STEW

A lamb stew is made like other stews. Some folks do not like the lamb cubes browned; others do—those are the brown gravy people—so take your pick. Then add the vegetables, carrots, onions, celery, potatoes and herbs and cook until the vegetables are just tender, not mushy.

LAMB ON SKEWERS

These are wonderful indoors and out, and always impart a note of gaiety to the simplest meal. Use strong steel skewers from eight to ten inches long.

Two pounds of lamb cut in squares and placed in a marinade for about eight to ten hours.

Marinade:

1 cup cider vinegar	½ cup olive oil
1 bay leaf	2 cloves garlic
parsley and oregano	tomato slices

Mix vinegar and oil and add herbs, which should be cut so all their goodness can seep out. Arrange a slice of lamb and one of tomato with a small onion next if you like onions on skewers. Broil over hot charcoal or under broiler flame, turning so the meat cooks evenly. If eating outdoors, serve with paper cups filled with cooked rice.

LAMB CHOPS

Lamb chops are easily broiled under a low flame and served hot with vegetables. If you want a change but still want lamb chops, why not lay a rice stuffing between two chops and slowly bake until done. Or arrange the dressing and place the chops in a heavy skillet or casserole and slip into the oven to bake slowly.

HONEY MINT SAUCE

1 cup honey   ½ cup tart apple cider
½ cup chopped fresh mint, using only the leaves

Heat honey with cider, add chopped mint, simmer for five minutes. Use this to baste lamb chops or roast, also place a bowl of sauce on the table.

LAMB AND CABBAGE ROLLS

1 medium head of cabbage	1 cup fresh tomatoes
4 pounds of lamb chopped rather coarsely	½ lb. ground pork
	oregano
1 cup raw rice	2 small onions

Cut the bottom core out of the head of cabbage, and trim the core deeply in a circle with a sharp knife. Place cabbage in boiling water and let stand five minutes. Mix tomatoes with rice, meats, onions, and herbs. Mix well and allow rice to soak up the tomato juice.

Remove gently the wilted leaves from the head of cabbage. Place a spoonful of the rice mixture in center of larger leaves and roll up. Cut up another fresh tomato and spread on bottom of baking dish. Lay cabbage leaves—filled—closely together so they will not unroll, and add enough water just to cover, or if you have plenty of fresh or home canned tomatoes, lay more tomatoes over the cabbage. Cover and simmer slowly or bake in slow oven for two hours.

LAMB CURRY

2 lbs. lamb cubed   1 tablespoon chopped onion
3 tablespoons oil   2/3 teaspoon curry powder
¼ cup chopped celery   2 tablespoons chopped parsley

Heat the oil and brown the lamb and onions. Cover with one cup boiling water, add all the other ingredients and simmer until meat is tender—about a one-half hour or so. Serve with steamed rice. The pan gravy may be thickened and poured over the rice.

LAMB PIE

2 lbs. ground lamb   ½ lb. sliced mushrooms
½ cup chopped onion   ½ cup chopped celery
1 teaspoon oregano   1 teaspoon basil
1 cup fresh or home canned tomatoes

Brown ground lamb with onion, add tomatoes and herbs, heat thoroughly. Lay mixture in oblong baking dish, add vegetables and sliced mushrooms. Cover the mixture with mashed potatoes and bake one hour.

Chicken

The broad term chicken should be broken down to:

Broiler, meaning a young bird not over 12 weeks old, or weighing more than two and one-half pounds.

These are best for broiling as the name implies. Half a bird is usually enough for one person and often more than enough.

Fryers can be 20 weeks old and heavier than the broiler by a pound or more. Generally they have full meaty breasts and having more fat can be roasted.

Roasting chickens are good for casseroles and fricassee. At this stage they are from five to ten months old, and can be male or female. Just be sure the breast bone is soft and pliable, which means it should be tender.

A fowl means a mature hen—the older girls—so to speak. It does require long slow cooking, but you gain flavor from a mature bird. These are best cut up; it makes it easier to cook all the goodness from the bones that way.

Capons are the unsexed birds, between six months to a year old. Since they become slow and inactive, their flesh is very tender, making a good roast.

MARINATED CHICKEN

The following marinade is enough for two broilers, which have been split, making four servings: Mix one cup olive oil, one-quarter cup chopped onion, one tablespoon apple cider vinegar, three tablespoons chopped parsley, one tablespoon tarragon. Sprigs of mint if you like mint—we do! Place broilers skin down in the marinade and let stand one hour before turning. Turn and allow other side to lay in marinade one hour. Then place on broiler with the drier side up, baste with marinade while broiling.

BAKED BROILERS

Split broilers, wash and rub insides with oil. Fill the cut side with stuffing of your choice—such as brown rice. Place skin side down in greased dish, cover and bake at 350° for about an hour. Garnish with sprigs of parsley, which should be eaten with the chicken.

CHICKEN WITH MUSHROOMS

2-3 pound broiler or frying chicken
¼ cup tart apple cider
6 tablespoons oil

4 small white onions chopped
chopped parsley
½ cup mushrooms

Cut the frying chicken into quarters, and season it. Heat oil and quickly brown the chicken on both sides. Cover, turn the flame low and cook for about 10 minutes. After 15 minutes of total time, add chopped onions, and the mushrooms and the tart cider and cook about 15 minutes more. Serve with brown rice.

CHICKEN CACCIATORA
OR
HUNTERS' SAUCE

This calls for a fowl, the original recipe called for wild fowl, ducks, and other birds. Rabbits were and can be cooked by this rule.

4 or 5 pound fowl
½ cup chopped onions
½ cup tart apple cider
1 bay leaf
¼ teaspoon oregano

½ cup olive oil
2 pounds tomatoes
½ teaspoon basil
¼ teaspoon marjoram

Saute' the pieces of chicken in oil until golden. Add the onions and let them cook a bit, then add tomatoes, and all other ingredients. Cover and cook slowly for one hour or more, depending on the age of the fowl and its tenderness. For the last half hour of cooking, have the cover partially open to allow the sauce to thicken as it cooks down.

BROILERS WITH HERBS

Chop 1 cup parsley ¼ cup onions
1 tablespoon sweet basil 6 tablespoons oil

From the neck end of the broiler, very carefully run a sharp knife between the meat of the breast and the breast bone. Be careful you don't pierce the skin. Mix the herbs well with oil, and with a small spoon and your fingers stuff each broiler half with the mixture so the flesh of the breast is completely covered. Brush the outside of the chicken well with oil, and broil three inches from the flame. Cook about 15 minutes; depending on size, turn carefully. This is worth your trouble if you've heard the phrase, "chicken breasts are dry," once too often. This will prove different.

CHICKEN FRICASSEE

To fricassee is to simmer. This method is used for veal and rabbit besides chicken. Just how you go about it is more or less a personal matter. Some folks put the meat right into the boiling water. Others want to brown the cut pieces in oil. And there are those who simply must boil it first and brown in oil later. Take your choice—it's mainly a matter of how "mother did it." After doing what you prefer with the meat, add one onion, one-half cup celery, parsley, basil and thyme, along with several carrots. Add three cups boiling water, simmer covered but with the top ajar until chicken is tender, one hour or so. If you like—strain and thicken the broth for gravy.

TURKEY

Turkey is cooked much the same as chicken so there won't be too much said about turkey that isn't already known. I'll pass on the advice which a delightful grandmother said to a young bride about to go marketing for her first Thanksgiving turkey: "Turkeys like women are best judged by their legs, honey; only with turkeys, it's mainly their feet." Her point was this: old turkeys have grayish colored feet, young birds have black feet, and the three-year-old has pinkish feet. When buying a turkey plan on a pound per person.

A turkey must be well washed before stuffing and do not overpack the stuffing, allowing swelling room. And remember, if you are using a hot stuffing you must cook the turkey at once. If the entire stuffing is cold, by that I mean not even the onions have been browned, then it's a bit safer to stuff in advance, if you must.

There are people who will stuff the same turkey with several different stuffings. The neck may hold one favorite dressing, the body another. Roast the turkey uncovered at 300° allowing 25 minutes per pound if the turkey is under 15 pounds, and 20 minutes a pound if over that weight, three and four pound turkeys can be split and broiled, as you do chickens; allow about 45 minutes.

66

CHESTNUT DRESSING

Two pounds of chestnuts which have been cut through the skins and boiled until tender.

Wheat germ, chopped parsley, chopped celery and seasonings to taste. Or use five to six cups cooked brown rice in place of wheat germ and season as usual.

It makes no difference what kind of dressing you make—just make sure you make it in large batches.

DUCK AND GOOSE

Goose and duck are cooked the same way, by slow cooking at 325°, allowing 25 minutes per pound. Be sure the duck or goose rests on a roasting rack so it will not be resting in its own melted fat. Pour off the fat while cooking, and if the birds are quite fatty, prick the breast with a fork to release the melted fat.

Some folks don't care to stuff a duck or goose with the traditional stuffings. If that's the case, just place a sliced onion, a few celery stalks, and a sprig of parsley right into the cavity. After the duck or goose is cooked, these may be discarded.

PANNED DUCKLING

Have duck cut into serving pieces and place on rack in roaster. Place water in bottom of pan, but don't let it come up to the meat on the rack. Cover and cook about 45 minutes over moderate heat, turn pieces once. Serve hot with vegetables. If possible use mushrooms as one of the vegetables. Duck steamed this way is very good to use in casserole dishes or salad.

Fish

"I go a fishing—for meat from the depths of the water."

Mention fish or fish chowder and someone is bound to ask: "What's Bouillabaisse?"

The answer is best given by the words of Thackeray from his Ballad of Bouillabaisse.

> "This Bouillabaisse a noble dish is,
> a sort of soup, or broth, or brew.
> A hotch-potch of all sorts of fishes
> That Greenwich never could out do.
> Green herbs, red peppers, mussels, saffern
> Soles, onion, garlic, roach, and dace;
> All these you eat at Terre's tavern,
> In that one dish of Bouillabaisse."

To the ambitious, I'll give the recipe for this famous dish.

BOUILLABAISSE

12 oz. of onions	2 cloves; stuck in the onions
1 oz. parsley	2 laurel leaves
1 spray of thyme	2 outer skins of a clove of garlic
1 oz. of shallots	2 oz. carrots
6 lbs. of any kinds of fish,	4 oz. of oil
such as soles, whiting,	¾ oz. of salt
barbe, plaice, etc.	¾ oz. of all spice
1 pinch of pepper	1 teaspoonful of powdered saffron
3½ pints of water	

MODE:—Cut the fish into long pieces of fillets, and place all the ingredients, except the saffron, in the saucepan in order as arranged; cover the pan closely, and boil for about 25 minutes. If whiting are cooked, they must be added after the other ingredients have boiled 15 minutes. Then remove the fish; drain carefully, and take off any particles that may adhere to them from the soup. Dress them high on a dish covered with a napkin. Strain the soup, add the saffron, pour into the tureen. Serve the fish at the same time as the soup.

NOTE: Bouillabaisse can be made of fresh-water fish, but is not so delicious as when made with sea-fish. It is of southern origin and ought to be a highly seasoned dish. This soup is well-known to all readers of Thackeray, by reason of his ballad wherein, visiting Paris when an old fogey, he recalls his remembrances of younger and more jovial days.

BUYING FISH

If buying fish at the fish market, there are a few things to look for to be sure the fish is fresh. Fish must be as fresh as possible to be good, which means the eyes are bright, the flesh firm and a fresh smell. One pound of fish with fins and tails serves two. Have the fish seller dress the fish for broiling or making fillets. To take the odor of fish from your hands, rub with vinegar or lemon juice. If you don't want the odor lingering on your cooking utensils, wash them in water with vinegar or lemon. Do not overcook fish; it should be cooked only until it loses its "shiny" look. Thaw frozen fish before cooking; if cooked frozen, it may become a bit tough.

BROILED MACKEREL

Have a mackerel split for broiling and rub the broiler with oil. Place fish skin down and let broil for about 20 minutes. Serve with Fennel Sauce. Mix together one tablespoon cornstarch and one cup cold water, add one tablespoon chopped fennel seeds. Simmer for a few minutes and serve over broiled fish. In an old book, I found that fennel seed was used to help digest the fat of the mackerel.

68

GREEN TROUT AND PERCH

These two fishes are best broiled and served with a Tartar Sauce, or Genoese Sauce.

GENOESE SAUCE

This is better with a more delicate fish, but also good on Perch.

1 tablespoon oil	2 tablespoons soy flour
1 cup tart apple cider	1 tablespoon chopped parsley
1 cup water	salt, pepper, nutmeg

Mix the oil and flour, add the tart cider and mix well; add the water and spices and simmer until it has cooked to about half the amount. This is good with boiled fish.

FILLET OF FISH

fillets of your choice	lemon juice
bread crumbs	seasoned soy flour

Sprinkle the fillets with lemon and roll in crumbs. Oil the broiler pan and broil four inches below the flame. Cook for 15 minutes and serve with lemon juice or Tartar Sauce.

STEAMED FISH

Some folks call this boiled fish, but please don't boil your fish—steam it! Place fish in colander over boiling water and cover. Figure about one minute of boiling time for each ounce of fish. Serve with lemon juice and olive oil or the sauce of your choice. Best fish to steam are red snapper, halibut, trout, whitefish, whiting, haddock, pollock and salmon, to name a few.

FILLET OF SOLE WITH MUSHROOMS

Steam one pound of fillet of Sole, then place in greased baking dish. Saute' one small onion in oil, add one-half pound mushrooms, pour over fish with two tablespoons of oil and bake at 375° until well heated and flavored.

BAKED STUFFED FISH

To stuff a fish well it should be between four and eight pounds. Stuff with your favorite stuffing and bake at 400° allowing 12 minutes per pound. The best stuffed fish I ever had was stuffed with sliced tomatoes, thinly sliced onion, parsley, green peppers and sweet basil. This really gives the flesh of the fish an excellent flavor. Bake as usual.

Whole fish baked include salmon, shad, sea trout, cod, swordfish and brook trout.

FILLETS BAKED WITH CAPERS

Lay fillets in oiled baking dish, sprinkle one-half cup of capers over the fish, dot with oil, sprinkle with lemon juice and bake at 375° for 30 minutes.

FISH BAKED IN TOMATOES

Cod or haddock is very good this way. Line baking dish with oil, add one cup tomatoes, dividing it in half, half over the fish, half under. The fish is baked between layers of tomatoes. Sprinkle with oregano, dot with oil, chopped onions, and bake at 375° for half an hour. Flavor with oregano and parsley.

Meatless
Dishes

In these meatless dishes we found herbs made the use of salt quite unnecessary. Try them.

ASPARAGUS LOAF

4 cups steamed cut up asparagus	3 beaten eggs
¼ cup wheat germ	2 tablespoons vegetable oil
1/3 cup cooked brown rice	1 cup of fresh tomatoes

Mix all ingredients well, bake in greased pan at 350°, 30 minutes.

ARTICHOKE OMELET

1 package frozen artichoke hearts or 6 fresh hearts

¼ cup vegetable oil	4 eggs
2 tablespoons parsley	2 teaspoons sweet basil
¼ cup chopped onion	

Heat oil, add artichoke hearts which are sliced thin. Add seasonings and cook until light brown. Beat eggs, pour over artichokes, cook slowly over low heat until eggs are set. Fold the omelet in half and serve on hot platter with one teaspoon chopped parsley sprinkled over the top.

ARTICHOKES AND BROWN RICE

4 small artichokes	1 onion
1 tablespoon oil	1 teaspoon oregano
1 cup cooked brown rice	1 tablespoon parsley

Remove the outer leaves of the artichokes and soak in water with lemon juice for half hour. Mix the other ingredients with the cooked rice. Spread the leaves of the artichokes and stuff the rice mixture around the inner leaves. Place upright in pan, add one and one-half cups of water, cover and cook 45 minutes or until outer leaves pull away from the bottom easily.

BEETS WITH YOGHURT

Slice beets very thin or grate, place in steamer over boiling water, add the beet tops along with a bay leaf, a sprig of parsley and one of basil. Let steam over boiling water for about five minutes. Remove the bay leaf, place beets in dish. Mix one-quarter cup of yoghurt with one teaspoon of honey, pour over beets and serve.

SWEET-SOUR CABBAGE

4 cups red cabbage shredded   2 onions
juice of 2 lemons   4 tart apples unpeeled
3 tablespoons honey   ¼ cup tart cider
1 tablespoon caraway seeds, one whole clove

Mix all ingredients, cook gently for about 10 minutes.

CABBAGE-RICE CASSEROLE

1 head of cabbage steamed   4 tablespoons
  and chopped   apple cider
1 cup cooked brown rice   1 teaspoon fennel seed
1 tablespoon chopped parsley   ½ cup chopped nuts

Oil a baking dish, line the bottom with half of the chopped cabbage. Lay the cooked rice, nuts and seasoning over the cabbage, moisten with two tablespoons of apple cider. Add another layer of cabbage, then the rice and nuts and the cider. Lay several coarsely chopped apples on top and bake for about 30 minutes at 325°.

CREOLE DISH

4 large zucchini squash   3 green peppers
6 large fresh tomatoes   ½ cup olive oil
3 sweet onions   ½ teaspoon sweet basil
½ teaspoon oregano

Slice onions and cook in oil until golden brown. Wash squash but do not peel unless a bit tough. Cut in one-half inch slices, arrange in layers with peppers, onions, oregano and tomatoes, lay sprigs of basil on the tomatoes. Bake slowly for about 30 minutes.

EGGPLANT LOAF

3 cups steamed eggplant, mashed 1 egg
¼ cup oil   1 cup chopped celery
1½ cups wheat germ   ½ teaspoon sweet basil
¼ cup tomatoes   ½ teaspoon oregano

Mix egg with mashed eggplant, add seasonings. Soak wheat germ in tomatoes, add eggplant mixture. Blend well, pour into greased baking dish. Bake at 350° for 30 minutes. Serves four-six.

POTATO LOAF

2 cups cooked potatoes   1 chopped green pepper
½ cup chopped celery stalks   1 egg
  and leaves   1 teaspoon chopped parsley

Blend all together until well mixed. Bake at 375° for 30 minutes or until brown. Serve with onion sauce.

CARROT CUTLETS

2 cups cooked brown rice	1 cup cooked mashed carrots
1 tablespoon onion	1 tablespoon soy milk
5 tablespoons vegetable oil	1 egg
1 tablespoon chopped parsley	¾ cup wheat germ

Mix rice and carrot pulp, add beaten egg and soy milk. Add other ingredients, form into cakes and roll in wheat germ. You can fry them in hot oil or grease a baking sheet with oil and bake the cutlets in a hot oven at 425° turning once. Brown and serve with chopped parsley.

ONION SAUCE

8 onions	1 tablespoon soy flour
1 tablespoon oil	juice of 1 lemon

Steam the onions over boiling water until tender. Mash or if you like a smooth sauce press through a sieve. Blend oil, flour and stir well. Add onions and cook gently for 10 minutes stirring until smooth. Add the lemon juice and serve with the potato loaf.

SPINACH LOAF

1 cup cooked brown rice	1 egg
1 cup celery, stalks and	2 cups cooked spinach
leaves chopped	wheat germ

Chop spinach, add rice and other ingredients. Pour into greased loaf pan, sprinkle with wheat germ. Bake at 400° for 30 minutes. Swiss chard may be used in the place of spinach for a change.

CASSEROLE OF VEGETABLES

1 cup uncooked brown rice	1 cup peas
1 cup tomatoes	4 potatoes sliced thin
1 onion sliced thin	basil and oregano
1 teaspoon chopped parsley	

Put all ingredients into casserole with four cups of stock or make it four cups of tomatoes, plus the first cup. Cover and bake in slow oven 300° until rice is tender. Serves four-six.

SPLIT PEAS WITH RICE AND TOMATOES

2 cups split peas soaked overnight	1 tablespoon chopped parsley
2 tablespoons oil	1½ cups uncooked brown rice
6 onions sliced thin	2 cups tomatoes
1 teaspoon sweet basil	1 teaspoon oregano

Soak peas overnight; add tomatoes, brown rice, onions which have been browned in oil, and herbs. Simmer until rice is tender, stirring often. Do not boil.